Ask the Black Bear Guides

Ask the Black Bear Guides

By J. Y. Jones

SAFARI PRESS INC.

An imprint of Globe Pequot, the trade division of
The Rowman & Littlefield Publishing Group, Inc.
4501 Forbes Blvd., Ste. 200
Lanham, MD 20706

Distributed by NATIONAL BOOK NETWORK

Jones, J. Y

ISBN 978-1-57157-282-0

Library of Congress Catalog Card Number: 2007929027

∞™ The paper used in this publication meets the minimum requirements of American National Standard for Information Sciences—Permanence of Paper for Printed Library Materials, ANSI/NISO Z39.48-1992

Dedication

As one writes more and more books, writing the dedication section becomes increasingly difficult because eventually you find that you have dedicated books to all the deserving parties you can bring to mind. Fortunately, however, I am not out of candidates yet. I hereby dedicate *Ask the Black Bear Guides to* America's black bear guides, black bear hunters, and the state and provincial wildlife departments that manage those magnificent animals so well.

Black-bear numbers have now grown to more than a million animals continent-wide, and neither animal-rights fanatics nor strict protectionists can claim one iota of the credit. Much praise and recognition rightfully go to the people on the front lines, those doing the scientific research and setting science-based quotas that remove only a very small percentage of the population—the harvestable excess that constitutes the essence of good management. On behalf of America's black bears, thanks should also go to working guides who insist on excellence in their camps, and on ethical hunters who respond in kind. Removing older, mature male black bears makes for a dynamic and booming population, with better cub survival. Hunting is the only legitimate and cost-effective way to accomplish that selective and highly beneficial thinning.

Black bears are the epitome of power and beauty in much of North America's natural world. They are a unique creation of the Majestic Glory, the triune God of Heaven and Earth, the result of a single creative act to produce an extraordinary animal, a mark of His handiwork. To Him also I dedicate this book, and to Him I commit my eternal destiny. To Him be all glory and praise.

Table of Contents

FOREWORD

This is a book that I wish J. Y. Jones had written thirty years ago in time for my first black bear hunt! I'm not complaining, but J. Y., where were you with this fine book when I needed the information it contained? I sure could have benefited from this book when that "giant" black bear walked out in front of me in that berry patch! Please forgive me Lord, but to me it looked big, to any first-time bear hunter, it would have looked big. . . . Although it was a boar, it wasn't nearly so "giant" as I thought. Welcome class, to black bear hunting 101.

And J.Y., where was this book fifteen years ago when I stood quaking and unable to make the call for my first black bear client? If this book had been available then, I'd have made the call with confidence and without fear. Instead, it was my client, Reed Williams, who came to my rescue that day by telling me, "It's a great spot to take that bear, and I'll be happy with it . . . so stop equivocating and cover your ears, I'm shooting." Would that all clients were so understanding about the inherent difficulties in guiding and outfitting for black bears.

I have hunted virtually every species of big-game animal in North America, I have had an outfitting business that has taken more than one thousand black bears, and I have personally guided hunters to more than three hundred black bears here on Vancouver Island in my own Pacific Rim Guide Outfitting territory, so I believe I am qualified to say that black bear hunting, black bear guiding and, more specifically, black bear judging are the toughest of any North American big-game hunting. Pardon the lack of humility, but in the opinion of this hunter/guide/outfitter, that is the reason this book needed to be written.

As with J. Y. Jones's other *Ask the Guides* books, this one is full of exactly the type of information that is beneficial to both a beginning and an experienced black bear hunter. The questions are to the point, and the answers, from some of North America's top bear guides and outfitters are poignant, concise, and dead on. Better still, the answers relate specifically to the local realities of each professional guide and outfitter.

Black bears are found from coast to coast and from nearly the bottom to nearly the top of this vast continent; they have the largest geographic distribution of any big-game animal in North America. Naturally, the actual hunting techniques used in Newfoundland will be very different from those used in Alberta. Here on Vancouver Island, in my outfitting territory, the spot-and-stalk regulations make for an inherently different black bear hunting adventure than what a black bear hunter might experience in Maine. The task of encompassing so much information from so many varied geographical locations, each with its own specific parameters, had to have been an onerous one, yet here is the book, complete and nearly encyclopedic on this diverse and challenging topic.

But this is far more than just a book of "hands-on" information about black bears: This book also addresses the issue of client/guide/outfitter relationships. The age of outfitted hunting is nigh because more hunters have more disposable income yet less time than ever. These hunters, consequently, are opting for the outfitted hunt these days more than ever before. Bear hunters are not the exception and may, in fact, be the rule in this regard. Black bear hunts are presently the most affordable big-game hunts in the world, but that said, being a black bear client comes with a responsibility. The top black bear guides in this book outline those responsibilities for you.

Yes, as I said at the beginning, I wish J. Y. had written this book years ago, and, yes, I wish this edition had been around way back when I was a green-behind-the-ears black bear hunter and black bear guide/outfitter, but as that saying goes, better late than never. Amen, and thank you J. Y. Jones.

Jim Shockey
www.jimshockey.com

Introduction and Acknowledgments

This book is the third in a series, the first two being *Ask the Elk Guides* and *Ask the Whitetail Guides*. It was natural for me to move on next to black bears since they are found throughout Canada except for the Arctic regions, in forty-one states of the United States, and in Mexico, making them the most widely distributed major predator on the continent. Some 40,000 to 50,000 black bears are legally killed by sport hunters each year, while the population of the species continues to expand. A hunt for black bears is, for many hunters, their first encounter with an animal that could be termed "dangerous." It is my hope that this book will give first-time black bear hunters, as well as veterans, added insights into the hunting of this wary and worthy game animal.

Early in the planning of this book, Ludo Wurfbain and I decided to organize the volume a little differently from the previous two books. There are essentially three types of hunting for black bears in North America: bait hunting, hound hunting, and spot-and-stalk hunting. Each requires its own approach, and each holds its individual challenges and difficulties. Instead of dividing up the continent into regions, as we had done in the past, we decided to divide our look at black bear hunting into these three categories, selecting four guides who conduct hunts by each method, and covering as wide an area as possible. I do hope that the result will make for fascinating reading.

I am indebted to many people for assisting me in compiling this book. Most of all, the featured guides have my gratitude, for submitting to the required interview and for sending me so many fine photos for inclusion. The search for the best guides was not perfect, and doubtless some of the best were overlooked. These twelve, however, are certainly a representative cross-section of the top black bear guides in North America. The people who offered names of guides for inclusion here include some of the top figures in the hunting and writing industry: Jim Shockey (himself a highly experienced bear guide, and the author of the foreword for this book); Scott Rupp; Diana Rupp; Jack Atcheson,

Jr.; Jerome Knap; Brent Sinclair; Don Causey; and John Zent. Many of my friends in Safari Club International also suggested the names of guides, including Dick Stockmar, Grant Adkisson, Tim Farren, Jim Gross, Alberto de Jongh, Glen Coolahan, Mike Schweibert, Bill Stratton, and Eric Albus. Of course, not all of the many guides suggested could be selected for inclusion, so I settled on those qualified guides who were most enthusiastic about participating. At the same time, I tried hard to select a wide geographic representation.

I sincerely hope that the efforts of the featured guides, as well as my own, have produced a book worth owning, and worth consulting when you are considering a black bear hunt in North America.

Note to readers: J. Y. Jones can be reached at www.jyjones.com.

The author with a 525-pound black bear he shot in North Carolina.

Chapter 1

MEET THE BLACK BEAR GUIDES

It is with great pleasure that I introduce black bear hunters everywhere to perhaps the best assemblage of black bear guides ever featured in one piece of literature.* From the youngest to the oldest, these guides are the most experienced group imaginable, and each has guided for an average of more than twenty-five years. Most are still actively outfitting and guiding, though a couple of them have ceased taking paying hunters and now hunt only for themselves. Whichever the case, all have a wealth of information to share, and what they have to say may open your eyes to a whole new world with respect to guide-client relations. I believe that anyone who has ever been guided on a black bear hunt will find himself described somewhere in the pages of this book.

These guides share a large number of characteristics in common. They universally place a high premium on hunter ethics, honesty, integrity, hard work, patience, dependability, and persistence. They all desire their hunters to come well prepared in every possible way, and they go into great detail delineating how one goes about doing this. Despite the commonality of such thoughts, their individual words are unique and different, so the reader never gets bored.

These guides are truly excellent representatives of the outdoor fraternity, and I think you'll agree they all offer invaluable insights into the world of black bear hunting. I can't think of a sufficient way to repay them for imparting their wealth of experience to us, the black bear hunters of today, so thank them yourself when you see them . . . and enjoy the information here to the utmost!

**Each guide can be found here in the sequence they appear in the book, with a brief summary of their backgrounds and experience, contact information, and a recent photograph. The material included here is taken directly from interviews with the guides and some cases from printed material they supplied. Most information in this book has been obtained by means of telephone interviews with each guide, and is essentially as they said it.*

Joe Jakab
Point Blank Hunts
527 McNeilly Road
Pittsburgh, PA 15226
www.pointblankhunts.com

Joe Jakab had a childhood dream to become a first-rate bear guide. Joe's parents emigrated from Hungary in 1956, and his first language is Hungarian. His parents died when he was only ten years old, and Joe was raised by a couple who were distant relatives.

Joe first hunted bears during the spring of 1979 on a cheap fly-in affair to Ontario that cost only a few hundred dollars. The only preparation made for his hunt was a couple of frozen sheep carcasses hung around a remote lake, but there were no bears hitting any of the baits.

After a few days of frustration, Joe, only eighteen at the time, decided to row across the lake in a canoe and still-hunt back to the cabin, around the end of the lake. He became hopelessly lost in the massive James Bay lowlands and was spotted from the air three days later. The following day he was picked up, bearing scars from black flies that would stay with him for over a year. But he had learned a vital lesson: The Canadian bush is big, and it's easy to get lost. It's best to be prepared—and to be cautious. Joe returned to hunt with another outfitter in the fall, but again there had been little preparation: Out of eight hunters, only one got a bear. Ironically, however, the outfitter was so impressed with Joe's enthusiasm that he hired him to work during the 1982 spring season. Later, Joe moved over to Shining Tree Camp, owned by Bob and Sue Evans in northern Ontario, an area on the edge of a huge wilderness. From these early experiences, as well as some good contacts with state biologists from several states and the U.S. federal government, he learned a great deal about bears.

A biologist named Dr. Lynn Rodgers, a man with a vast amount of black bear knowledge, was willing to let Joe visit him at his research center in Ely, Minnesota, and spend some time there studying black bear behavior. Joe took out his first paying hunters at age twenty-two in 1983, and he took six bears for seven bow hunters. He remembers looking up at the Northern Lights and thanking God for letting him be so blessed. He's now been in business for twenty-four seasons, and as of this writing he has taken 647 bears with clients in Ontario and Quebec, and another fifty or so in other provinces, as well as in Alaska and New Mexico.

For many years he has run two spring camps in Quebec with thirty-one licenses, a quota that has recently been raised to fifty-two. He also takes out twelve to eighteen hunters in Ontario in the late summer and early fall. Bear hunting is special to him because of the great sense of freedom he experiences in the Canadian wilderness. Joe revels in seeing spring breaking out in the bush, in setting baits in unexplored places, and the like. He reads the *Journal of Wildlife Management,* as well as all the books and articles he can find on black bear management and hunting.

Horace Lane
RiverRun Outfitting and Tours, Ltd.
P.O. Box 1450
Lewisporte, NL, Canada
A0G 3A0
709-535-8770
www.riverrunnl.com

Horace Lane started his own camp in 1990. The Wildlife Division in Newfoundland had wanted to harvest more black bears through the outfitting industry, but most outfitters felt that there was just not enough of a market for black bear hunts. Nevertheless, authorities allowed twelve new entrants into the outfitting business in the late 1980s and early 1990s, and Horace was one of those twelve. Thus it was a government decision on black bears that enabled him to get into the outfitting business full time.

Horace has a high school and postsecondary education, concentrating on the service industry. He grew up in Millertown, a small village in the center of Newfoundland with only about fifty families. In that small town, which had no organized sports or even a school gymnasium, there were, however, some seven outfitters—a very high percentage of the population. Hunting was a big industry in Millertown. Moose hunters came there from all over the United States, and Horace developed an interest even when he was still too young to participate. Horace learned the rules of firearm safety and hunting ethics from an early age, and in the process he became deeply interested in the outdoors. He now has four daughters, all of them good target shooters.

Over the past fifteen years, Horace's hunters have taken some 120 black bears. The logistics of getting to Newfoundland and the prices that Newfoundland outfitters must charge are contributing factors to keeping hunter volume low. The hunts are generally spring hunts, although Newfoundland outfitters do take some black bears in the fall, as the province has both spring and fall seasons. To Horace, what is special about black bear hunting is the opportunity to observe the animals up close, especially when hunting over bait. He finds that hunters can learn a lot about animals and their habits by watching them for extended periods—such as while on the stand.

Horace reads *Big Game Adventures, Safari, North American Hunter,* and *Petersen's Hunting.* He has not been a big fan of magazine hunting stories because it seems to him that he gets enough of hunting tall tales in camp!

Don Lind
South Peace Outfitters
P.O. Box 458
High Prairie, AB, Canada
T0G 1E0
780-523-4455
www.southpeacehunts.com

Don Lind began bowhunting bears over bait on his own property when it became legal in Alberta in the 1980s. Shortly thereafter he started guiding friends, and he began guiding professionally in 1998. Having grown up in northern Alberta, he had always had access to an abundance of wildlife. All of Don's big-game guiding occurs in Wildlife Management Unit 521, which is an area of some eighteen hundred square miles in the southern part of the Peace River region of northwestern Alberta.

Don has a postsecondary diploma in Wildlife Management, and he has used that education to help him manage his hunting area. He grew up hunting in the area where he now outfits, and he is raising two boys who love hunting and working with their father. Don has been married to his wife, Jackie, for eighteen years, and she is an integral part of the family business. Their company is very much family owned and operated, and it is run in conjunction with the Lind cattle ranch. Over the past eight years, Don's hunters have taken more than two hundred bears.

South Peace Outfitters is allocated twenty-four bear hunters per year, and each hunter is authorized to take two bears. Don does most of his hunting in the spring, although he does take some fall bear hunters, too. His season is normally a month long, from mid-May to mid-June, and he usually has six hunters in camp at a time. He never tires of black bear hunting and guiding, and he says that the spring season, one of the most beautiful times of year in northern Alberta, is a wonderful time to be working outdoors. He especially loves bear hunting because bears always exhibit unpredictable behavior and are a challenge to hunt.

He enjoys reading magazines with stories about hunting a variety of species, and he is working his way through this author's book *One Man, One Rifle, One Land*, which was given to him by a German hunter some time ago.

Claude Turcotte
1062 St-Paul
St-Rémi, QC Canada J0L 2L0
450-454-7975
www.bigbearhunt.com
bigbearguide@bigbearhunt.com

When Claude Turcotte was just six years old, he became fascinated by the woods and fields around his home. He had been a hunter at heart ever since that early age, hunting everything he could. His bear hunting began in earnest in an area four hours north of Montreal, a truly wild area, and it was that experience that convinced him bear hunting would be his life's work. Claude had a friend who had guided for bears for a long time, and that friend introduced him to the activity. He was hooked from the beginning, back in the 1980s. Claude started guiding with his friend, and he's been bear hunting ever since.

Claude's forte is that he has always put a strong emphasis on guiding—not for just any bear, but for really big bears. He started his own guiding business thirteen years ago, and at that point he stopped all other work so as to concentrate on guiding. He has two boys, only six and four years of age, and they have already started helping him with various duties around the camp.

Claude's hunters have taken at least five hundred bears—probably more like six or seven hundred. Additionally, he takes another twenty or so that are nuisance bears. Claude guides between fifty and sixty hunters per year in his camps. He states that black bear hunting is special to him because of the adrenaline rush that a hunter gets when a bear is coming in, and that uncertain feeling of not knowing exactly what is going to happen next. He believes that no other game of any kind gives you quite that kind of feeling. As a guide, the challenge and thrill is to figure out exactly where and how to get the biggest bears, as well as planning out a program so that his hunters get a chance at a real trophy.

Claude says that there is very little in the literature in his native French, so he reads all that he can get his hands on about bears in the English language. He does note that sometimes what he reads seems a joke to him, an obvious attempt by an author to promote a particular outfitter's operation because the author was given a free hunt, or something of the sort. He dislikes stories that make bear hunting over bait sound as though it is the greatest adventure in the world, which he readily admits it is not. However, he does say that it is fun and relaxing. In many articles, he says, the danger and the exploits are regrettably overblown.

Wayne Bosowicz
Foggy Mountain Guide Service
131 Ladd Road
Sebec, Maine 04481
www.foggymountain.com
info@foggymountain.com

Wayne Bosowicz has been in the business of hunting bears in Maine since 1964. He has worked closely with state biologists in Maine, and has done a lot of volunteer work with them. Wayne belongs to the International Association of Black Bear Biologists, and he has studied the animals intensively. He's been a regular at seminars all over North America, and he has even talked to Russian biologists, and to the Americans who are experts on the panda.

Wayne has been married to his wife, Donna, for a long time, and they have one boy and one girl. His son was forced to leave their bear hunting business five years ago and take up another line of work when Ontario closed the spring bear season, which accounted for 65 percent of his family's income. Wayne states that it's not possible even to think about how many bears his hunters have taken. Some years it's into three figures, he says, so the total must be in the thousands. Wayne has been guiding for forty-one years, so a little simple multiplication makes his contention plausible. He states, tongue in cheek, that if he dies and goes to heaven, he sure hopes there isn't a bear up there waiting for him at the gate!

Wayne notes that what is most special about black bear hunting is the sheer unpredictability of the animal. He recites the one-liner that the only thing predictable about a bear is its unpredictability, and maintains that the old saying is certainly true. While there is a vast body of information on black bears,

Wayne feels that what biologists know—and what all professional bear hunters know—could be stored in a thimble—compared with the amount there is to know.

Every year he learns more. Wayne is featured as a hound guide in this book, but he actually learned a lot more about bears by baiting them than he did as a hound hunter. While he does mostly bait hunts these days, he feels that he knows as much as anyone about hunting bears with hounds. However, he says that it is when you're baiting bears that you really learn about them because then you have to get into their minds.

Wayne guides throughout all of Maine and Ontario. Among his favorite books is Richard T. Smith's *Book of the Black Bear*, a wellspring of reliable information.

Wade Lemon
P.O. Box 222
235 South 100 West
Holden, UT 84636
435-795-2299
www.tristateoutfitters.com
wlemon@crystalpeaks.com

Wade Lemon guides mostly in Utah, but he does quite a bit of hunting on a couple of Indian reservations as well, where you can avoid the mandatory Utah draw and simply buy tags over the counter. Wade has been running dogs since he was eleven years old. He had a buddy who was thirteen at the time, and the two of them used to take the pickup and go hunting along the back roads of the ranch, initially for lions. He and his friend found a big lion track in fresh snow one day, and their dogs wouldn't do a thing with it. The two boys walked the track until they spotted the lion—and then the dogs took off and treed it. They figured at that point that they were the best lion men around, and had the best dogs.

Utah is tough country for hunting bears with dogs, holding some of the biggest and meanest dog-fighting bears in the world, and it took Wade several years to catch his first bear. Eventually he became good at it, though, and he's been taking paying hunters out since about 1979. Wade's ancestors for generations had been ranchers near Ferron, Utah, the first white people to settle in that part of the world. It's an area with a lot of bears and a lot of cougars. Wade learned much from the state bear hunter, Phillip Taylor, when he was growing up, as well as from Kim Payne, another state bear and lion hunter. A famous bear hunter from California, George Flournoy, came along years later and completed Wade's education in the subject.

Wade takes ten to twenty bear hunters a year, five to ten on Utah tags and the rest on the Indian reservations. His total take would be several hundred over the years, but he's not sure of the exact number. He admits that his number of bears taken isn't particularly impressive, but he takes a lot of very big bears. He has only one or two hunters in camp at a time; he doesn't like mixing parties of hunters, but he will take up to four at a time in one party.

Hound hunting for bears in Utah is a special challenge, with big, rough country and big, rough bears. One thing that intrigues Wade is how bears learn through association, more than any other animal he's ever hunted. He notes that bears are certainly smart animals that learn quickly about hunters and their dogs. Wade isn't a big reader, but he says that he is an expert at reading bear sign!

Jerry E. "Finn" Nykanen
187 12½ Avenue
Turtle Lake, WI 54889-8851
715-986-4488

Finn Nykanen started hunting bears back in the 1950s, when you didn't even need an extra license to shoot one; they were included on the deer license. Up until around 1960 or so, the state paid a one hundred dollar bounty on bears, and people trapped them with leg-hold traps for the bounty. Finn remembers one lady who trapped a bear so big that the local men had to get a horse to drag it out. In 1974 the first bear licenses were issued in Wisconsin. Finn hunts in Bayfield County, Wisconsin, which runs right up to Lake Superior. He learned about black bear hunting simply by hunting them. He's been a farmer all of his life, and hunting is an important part of life for his family.

Finn and his wife, Shirley, have four children, and all of them are hunters, even the three girls. Finn's son is an avid hound hunter, too, and keeps his own pack of dogs. They go hunting whenever somebody draws a bear tag, and now even their grandchildren are putting in for them. Hound hunting runs deep in their family: Finn's twenty-two-year-old grandson also keeps dogs, and he's especially fond of black bear. One of Finn's granddaughters is going to school to become a game warden.

Most years Finn and his hunters take ten to fifteen bears with hounds. Over the years he's taken hundreds, although he can't say exactly how many. Finn is an oddity in this book, however, because he takes out no hunters for money. All of his hunters are people who have drawn a bear tag and know about him and his dogs. As a result, he states, "We usually keep a full house up here during bear season." Finn takes as many as twenty-five hunters, depending on how many of the people who know about him draw a tag.

In his younger days he did a lot of raccoon hunting with hounds, but black bear gave him more return for his efforts—and that's one of the things he sees as special about bear hunting. A raccoon may take a couple of runs around a cornfield before treeing, but a black bear might run half an hour or eight hours—you just never know. Finn believes that the quality of the bear dogs is the primary factor in how far a bear will run before treeing.

Finn is a life member of the NRA, and he reads all their publications.

Mike Richie
26 Haynes Creek Road
Salmon, ID 83467
208-756-3231
richieoutfitting@centurytel.net

Mike Richie grew up in the hunting business because his father was an outfitter for more than fifty years. The older Richie always had hounds for bear hunting, so it's somewhat of a family tradition. Mike guides in the Selway-Bitterroot Wilderness Area of Idaho. He has been hunting bears and cougar with hounds in there for many years, primarily in the Moose Creek area. He grew up in Darby, Montana, on the Montana side of the Selway, and thus has spent pretty much his entire life in the Selway. His father's area was on the Montana side, and after he sold his area, Mike was able to procure his own.

Mike now has a son who graduates from high school this year, and he wants to join his father in the guiding business. Mike's wife, Dawn, is from an outfitting family, too, with an outfitter father. She helps out with all aspects of the business—cooking, packing, shuttling stock around—and even does some of the guiding. She's Mike's right hand, and he readily states that he couldn't carry on this business without her. Mike has taken between four and five hundred black bears for his guided clients, and he takes about twenty hunters per year. Most of his hunts are spring hunts, just because the season is longer.

Mike views black bear hunting as pretty challenging compared with other types of hunting, and he says that it takes really good dogs to catch bears. Almost any dog will chase a mountain lion, he says, but it's different with bears: You need special dogs to be consistently successful because not every dog will give chase.

Mike isn't the first person to have noticed that really good bear dogs are not made, they're born. He says that bears are a lot of fun to chase, but it takes a different kind of person to hunt them with dogs in true wilderness. The hunt is physically demanding, and he believes that "challenging" may be too soft a word. A determined bear can run forever, and sometimes it takes a long time to catch up.

Mike reads all of the Safari Club International publications. He thinks that every hunter ought to be a member of that club because SCI does more to protect hunting rights than any other organization—whether you're a bear hunter, a deer hunter, or hunt in Africa, and whether you hunt with rifle, bow, handgun, or shotgun. He touts SCI because they stand up for everyone's rights, and he loves their magazine. He also reads *Bugle* and *North American Hunter.* As far as writing that's specific to bear hunting, he mentions a book by the most famous hound hunter of all time, Ben Lilly, called *The Ben Lilly Legend.*

Darren DeLuca
Vancouver Island Guide Outfitters
Box 1062, Station A
Port Alberni, BC, Canada
V9Y 7L9
250-724-1533
www.dfdeluca@shaw.ca

Darren DeLuca started guiding for black bears on Vancouver Island when he was twenty-four years old, more than twenty years ago. His father-in-law was in the guiding business, and Darren started helping out; eventually it turned into something he did full time. Darren didn't come from a family of hunters, but he did have uncles and cousins who hunted. He always knew that hunting was what he wanted to do. He had some friends who hunted, and that's where he got started, initially hunting deer. When his father-in-law got into the guiding business, Darren followed right along.

He's been married now for some seventeen years, and he and his wife have three daughters, one sixteen years old and twin fifteen-year-olds. He states that it's all trouble at his house!

Darren has taken about three hundred black bears while guiding. These days he doesn't take as many personally: He's now the outfitter, and his guides take most of the bears. The outfit takes between thirty and forty hunters a year. He takes twenty-four hunters in the spring, and another six or eight in the fall. His operation is in a two-bear area, so he waits to see how many two-bear hunters book in the spring so that he's not overbooked for the fall. His operation keeps a pretty good waiting list, so he can fill in as many hunters in the fall as his quota will allow.

Darren states that the really special thing about black bear hunting is that it's primarily a spring hunt, and on Vancouver Island the weather gets better and better and the days get longer in the spring. More bears are coming out all the time. Fall days on Vancouver, on the other hand, become progressively colder, darker, and rainier. He also likes hunting on salmon streams on the island because it's interesting to watch the bears, which become active in spring, walking around, catching salmon, and fighting.

His two favorite magazines are *Sports Afield* and *Petersen's Hunting.* He finds that most of the writers in those publications are fairly knowledgeable, and you don't get the exaggeration found in many other magazines.

Mark Galla
Alaska Peak and Seas
P.O. Box 362
Wrangell, AK 99929
907-723-2822/907-874-2454
www.wedoalaska.com
mark@wedoalaska.com

Mark Galla began guiding about 1987 for other outfitters for Dall sheep, caribou, and the like, and he did a lot of his work on the Alaska Peninsula. He gradually developed a desire to pursue guiding as his chosen profession, so he put in a lot of hours working to save enough to purchase the boats and equipment needed to get started. He's been a registered guide in the state of Alaska since 1990.

Mark's family moved to Alaska from Oregon in 1967 when he was seven or eight years old, at which time his father had gotten a job logging on Baranoff Island, where there was no shortage of brown bears. His mother taught Mark and his brother by means of a correspondence course until there were enough children on the island for the creation of a one-room school house. He left the island to attend high school in Wrangell, where he now lives.

He has personally guided between 125 and 150 hunters to black bears. All of Mark's hunts take place from his 53-foot yacht, which serves as a luxurious base camp. He generally takes two to four hunters per trip, and about twenty black bear hunters per year. He loves black bear hunting in this way because being based from a boat he can cover a huge area. Mark notes that if he finds himself in a spot that isn't meeting expectations, he can easily relocate camp to another bay several miles away.

For reading material, Mark likes *Petersen's Hunting, Big Game Adventures,* and the Safari Club International publications. Mark has four children, ages five to twenty-seven.

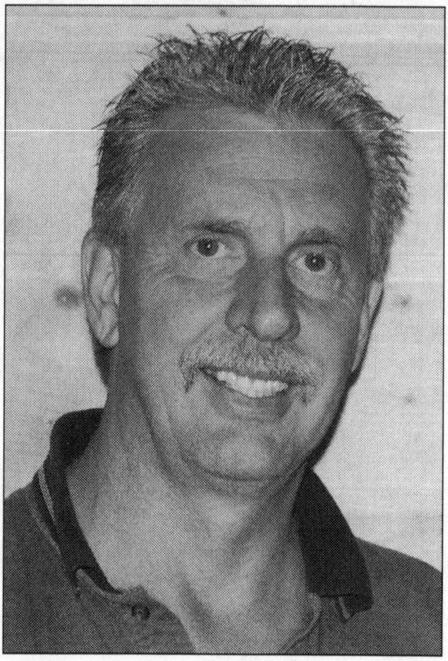

Kevin Olmstead
Pacific Bear Outfitters
P.O. Box 6677
Fort St. John, BC, Canada
V1J 4J1
250-789-9494
www.prophetmuskwa.com
kevin@prophetmuskwa.com

Kevin Olmstead's company has had an operation in northern British Columbia since 1986, so he has many years of guiding and outfitting experience for elk, moose, and mountain goat. A little later the company acquired a Stone sheep area in BC, and still later a Dall sheep area in the Yukon. They took the odd black bear up there but didn't offer hunts specifically for the species. Then, in 1999, they began guiding and outfitting for black bears in the Queen Charlotte Islands. He and his partners chose that location for a black bear operation specifically because the Queen Charlotte Islands are known to have some of the largest black bears in the world.

Kevin was born in 1955. He started out in the financial planning business in 1975, doing estate planning and pension and profit-sharing plans. All of his life, however, he's been an avid hunter, and he did a lot of it on his own before getting into the profession. A moose hunt in British Columbia in 1985 started a long relationship with that area. Kevin had some ideas on how to get into the outfitting business and provide upgraded services to clients, but he wanted to have several locations, so that repeat clients could come back and hunt a different species without changing outfitters.

Kevin and his wife, Victoria, have three children, and Victoria works hand in hand with him in the outfitting business. Theirs is truly a family business because the grown children, having been raised in the business, are active in various aspects of it. Kevin's son Sean is their pilot. Another son, Nathan, runs the farming and ranching operations, while Jamie, their daughter, lives in Seattle and does advertising and bookings for the company. They have recently built a lodge in the Queen Charlottes, and they also have a fly-in lodge in northeastern British Columbia.

Kevin estimates that he has taken about two hundred black bears for his clients. Last year his hunters shot about forty in the Queen Charlotte Islands. The company's goal is to increase that number each year by a little. The allowable harvest for their area, according to government figures, is 304 bears, so his hunting outfit has almost unlimited potential for expansion. Still, he states that what is most important is not the quantity of black bears taken but the quality. Kevin's goal as an outfitter is to find an area with exceptional black bear trophies and offering fine spot-and-stalk hunting. He felt that the Queen Charlotte Islands were a really good sleeper location, a place with virtually no hunting pressure, perfect habitat, and excellent genetics.

Kevin isn't a big reader, but he enjoys *Outdoor Life*, which is one of his favorite magazines.

Jimmie C. Rosenbruch
Glacier Guides, Inc.
P.O. Box 219
Gustavus, AK 99826
435-628-0973/907-697-2252
www.glacierguidesinc.com
jrosen@redrock.net

Jimmie Rosenbruch began his guiding career in Alaska forty-one years ago. He moved there just after statehood, and started out working for the government as an engineer. At first he used his vacation time to guide hunters for bears, and for a time he had all of southeastern Alaska to himself. Today, however, he counts about fifty outfitters there. He incorporated thirty-one years ago and operated as a sole proprietorship before that.

Jimmie says that he learned black bear hunting at the school of hard knocks. His family operation holds the largest allocation of black bear permits in Alaska because of their past use of the resource.

Jimmie has done a lot of international hunting, and he is easily the most celebrated active guide featured in this book. He received Safari Club International's Professional Hunter of the Year Award in 2000, and the C. J. McElroy Conservation Award prior to that. He was SCI's International Hunter of the Year in 2005, and he received the prestigious Weatherby Award in 2006.

He estimates conservatively that his hunters have killed between 1,200 and 1,500 black bears over the years, and he suspects that their operation has taken more bears—both brown and black—than any other in the world. Alaska's allocation of tags permits Glacier Guides to take as many as forty-eight bears, and they consistently guide approximately forty hunters, give or take.

To Jimmie, everything about black bear hunting is special. He notes that his operation gets hunters out into the field with good people in a unique area—the rain forests of southeastern Alaska—so it's a great all-round experience.

Jimmie is a real fan of the *Ask the Guides* series, of which this book is a part. He states that the books have as much merit as anything he's seen in a long time. His operation has had more than thirty major articles in all of the major hunting literature, and he has worked with Ruger, Swarovski, the NRA, and others. He also says that, although the articles have been well written, there are few really good sources of information on black bears. He agreed to participate in *Ask the Black Bear Guides* so as to help in providing such a resource.

Section I

HUNTING OVER BAIT

Chapter 2

SELECTING AN OUTFITTER/GUIDE FOR HUNTING OVER BAIT

What should a hunter look for when seeking a black bear outfitter/guide?

Joe Jakab: I'd look at the area first. Big bears need to reach a certain age in order to achieve their full potential, and that takes eight to fifteen years. I'd look for an area with little hunting pressure, and for outfitters who have areas adjacent to "bear reservoirs," such as large roadless areas or parks. Avoid areas with lots of easy access. Bears are overhunted in many places all over Canada, in my opinion. Talk to the outfitter and see if he really enjoys bear hunting, or if he does it just as a secondary operation. A lot of fishing camp operators in Ontario and Quebec offer bear hunts, but too often they have little interest in bears and little respect for what it takes to hunt them. I'd avoid anyone who lacks enthusiasm for bears. A good black bear guide will be not only enthusiastic but also knowledgeable about the animal.

Horace Lane: I think you should first get some idea of the area he hunts, how accessible it is, and so on. Accessibility is a very important factor, especially in a province like ours. I have one thousand miles of forest access road in my area, and that's a huge advantage over some areas. It's particularly true where you fly in. In most cases you have to walk to the hunting area, and there are only a limited number of places to hunt within walking distance of camp. Here, we can access our entire area with either four-wheel-drive trucks or ATVs. There should be low numbers of people in the area, too; I can count on the fingers of one hand the number of local residents who come into my area to hunt. Access is also extremely important when it comes to putting out the baits because without good access for vehicles,

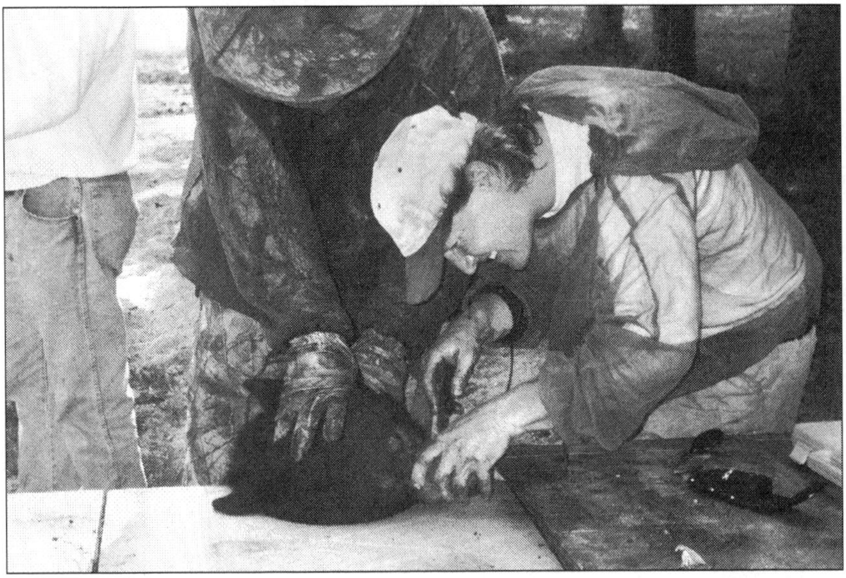

Trophy care and preparation is a major consideration. (Photo courtesy of Joe Jakab)

you simply can't do the job well. Some of my baits are seventy kilometers from our base camp, and that just won't work if you don't have good vehicle access. I can spread out my hunters and know for certain that they are hunting different bears—and that it's not the same bear hitting different baits. We have a big forestry industry in our area, and that's good for bears because it lends itself to second-growth vegetation. In Newfoundland, that means the land is heavy with blueberries, raspberries, grass, and other good food sources for bears.

Don Lind: First, I would look for an outfitter with a baiting area, such as Northern Alberta, in which he could provide me with an opportunity for two bears during my hunt. There is such a variety in bears that a two-bear hunt seems logical. You can take a black, chocolate, cinnamon, blonde, and so forth. If I were a first-time bear hunter, I would take an average-size bear first, and then continue my hunt for a larger bear, or one of a different color. The second thing I would research in depth would be the outfitter's reference list. I always suggest that prospective hunters ask an outfitter how many clients he takes per year.

Nice boar taken by Point Blank Hunts. (Photo courtesy of Joe Jakab)

Then, having obtained that information, ask him for his client list for the last two years. If the outfitter won't provide that information, he must be hiding something. I put a lot of emphasis on my past clients' experiences to help me sell my hunts.

Other questions that are very important are these: How many active bait sites are there per hunter? How much have those sites been hunted prior to the hunter's arrival? How much bait is used per site, and how often are the sites rebaited? I run a minimum of three active sites per hunter, but often I have four or five. The bait sites are all started a minimum of ten days prior to the hunt. That is important, so that several bears will visit the site. And each group of hunters will have access to some sites that have not yet been hunted that season.

I continually rotate bait sites to provide hunters with access to fresh sites, as well as to distribute the hunting pressure more evenly. Our sites are baited with a large volume of bait, so that all of the bears visiting have an opportunity to feed, and each site is rebaited at least every second day. We run such a large number of baits that it would be impractical to access each site daily. Bears are opportunists that will eat daily if possible, but they also have a stomach system which ensures that if they miss a meal or two, they can work off their reserves. It's been my experience that a bear will visit a bait site for several days to see if the site has been refreshed before giving up on it and moving on.

Some outfitters believe that using a small portion of bait entices the bears into the site early, giving the hunter a better chance earlier in the evening. Although that idea may have some merit, I believe that the early bear gets the grub—and that's usually the smaller bear. If the big one comes in and doesn't get something to eat, it moves on in search of another food source. Also, by feeding in volume and holding multiple bears at a site, you increase the chances of drawing a large boar in to a sow in heat.

Claude Turcotte: What I'm offering is exactly what hunters are looking for! I have the exclusive right to hunt in two of Quebec's largest wildlife preserves. The first thing to look at is the size of an outfitter's territory, and how many bears that outfitter will take out of his area. You have to be sure that the outfitter has complete control over how many bears are taken from his area, or you can be in trouble. An outfitter can have a fairly small area, take only a few hunters, and still do a good job. But if he's taking a lot of hunters into a small area every year, you probably won't see any big bears.

I'd look at how heavily the outfitter has been hunting an area, and also at how many years he's been there. After that, look into how he carries on his operation. There are some poor operators out there who have no idea how to fine-tune a bait to bring in big bears. One thing I'd add is that it's very important that each hunter be put on a virgin bait—one that nobody else has hunted that season. Make sure that your outfitter offers that as a guarantee.

What are (a) the most important single characteristic and (b) the worst possible deficiency in a black bear guide?

Joe Jakab: Enthusiasm is the most important single characteristic, and lack of it is the worst.

Camp conditions can vary widely. Make sure you know what you want. (Photo courtesy of Joe Jakab)

Horace Lane: Patience is the most important characteristic, from a number of standpoints. You have to be persistent to get bears even to come to a bait sometimes. It's a major deficiency if you lack the patience to train bears to come to the bait. Patience also spills over into your relationship with your hunters because if you're impatient with them you're just not going to give them the service or experience they deserve.

Don Lind: Bear baiting is a very laborious job! I think that the success of the hunt is directly proportional to the physical effort the guides put into baiting. Bear baits should be numerous and spaced over a large distance, so that the same bears aren't visiting different sites. Sites should also be remote and spread throughout the area, so that overharvesting is not a concern. Although large boars do travel a lot during the spring breeding period, they are territorial; the dominant bear is never forced out of his territory by a subdominant male. Covering that much territory is a lot of work, but the guide should be willing to work hard for his client and provide him with the best possible opportunity for an enjoyable and successful hunt. We also try to personalize our hunts to meet a client's special needs or requests, within reason. That includes things like placing a second stand for a spouse or parent/child hunting party, getting clients out before dark if requested, and the like. The guide needs to be flexible in order to provide the client with the most enjoyable experience possible.

Claude Turcotte: The guide really needs to know the bear, and that's the most important thing. Also, I'd say that it's important to have a calm nature, but I'm not that way myself. I'm always hyperactive! The worst guide is the one who books clients dishonestly, by making false promises. It's very hard to pick out a good outfitter for bears at a hunting show. I stopped doing shows because right next to my booth would be another outfitter, and I'd know that he was dishonest or overharvesting his area. The hunter has a hard time telling the difference between him and me, and I felt that I would be classed with that kind of guide if I kept going to such shows. One of my competitors has about twenty-five Web sites offering hunts for almost every animal in North America, and from the sites you would think he was

Make sure your outfitter prepares ahead of time for a baited hunt. (Photo courtesy of Don Lind)

the best in the world. But about all he has is a computer with all those Web sites, and that seems dishonest to me.

Baiting is hard but necessary work. (Photo courtesy of Claude Turcotte)

Is there any exceptional qualification for being a black bear guide that may not apply to other types of guiding?

Joe Jakab: He's got to be knowledgeable about the animal, probably more than when hunting any other kind of animal.

Horace Lane: One qualification goes back to the patience issue. Most guides in Newfoundland are used to moving around a lot, going from one place to another looking for moose, caribou, and so forth. If they don't find any, they move on to another place. With bears over bait, though, you've got to stay put, and it isn't easy for some guides to make the transition. Most of our hunters are on stand by themselves, but the guide is somewhere in the vicinity waiting for them to get their chance. That requires that the guide be as patient as the hunter, or more so.

Don Lind: Black bear baiting isn't rocket science. You need to establish a site that is in bear habitat, and the bears will come. But the guide must be willing to put in long, hard hours. Since most of our bears are taken out of the field after dark, the bear guide must be willing to track the bear down at night, even if it's only wounded. We try to locate our clients' bears before leaving the stand site for a couple of reasons. First, we have lost a couple of bears that we had to leave out overnight because other bears fed on the downed carcass. Second, since many of our sites are remote, it saves coming back in again the next day.

Claude Turcotte: That's a good question because the guide's most important work in bear hunting is done during the

Having a lot of bears is a big advantage! (Photo courtesy of Claude Turcotte)

three weeks before the hunter arrives. After that the guide can be just a sixteen-year-old kid who drops the hunter off at the bait. However, there is a special way one needs to operate at the bait because most often the bear will be within 100 or 150 yards. I'll explain how we do it in my operation a little later on.

What does a good black bear guide do to ensure safety while hunting a uniquely dangerous animal?

Joe Jakab: The only real danger to black bear hunting is following up when a bear is wounded. It's especially dangerous if the wounded bear, as rarely occurs, happens to be a sow with cubs. We walk our hunters in to the bait sites, and either my guides or I will lead all follow-up on bears that have been hit. We supply hunters with radios, and they're told to contact us thirty minutes after the shot.

Horace Lane: You've got to set down firm rules on what to do after the shot, and that's probably the most important safety issue. As the hunter, you're there alone; the guide is sitting aside

Preparing the trophy is a high priority in a quality camp. (Photo courtesy of Claude Turcotte)

somewhere, and he may not even hear the shot. You can't just get down and go after that animal alone, particularly when most of the opportunities come just as the light is fading. We don't want people wandering away from the stand looking for a bear at any time—but particularly not as it's getting dark. Wounded animals are dangerous animals, and that's especially true of bears. They might even stalk and hunt you. So we really lay down the law about waiting for the guide to get there, and we stress that he will be there pretty quickly after the shot.

Don Lind: The guide must be alert and aware of his surroundings at all times. He should never put his client at risk and should assume that the client is totally unfamiliar with bear habits. The guide must provide specific instructions and rules for the hunter to follow, and the hunters need to understand and follow those rules. There are numerous instances each year in which we encounter bears that have had no previous human encounters and have no respect for humans. Such bears can potentially be a problem.

Claude Turcotte: When my hunters come into camp, we have a long lunch and we talk about a lot of things, and safety is one of the things we cover. We try to explain to each hunter which direction to expect the bear to come from, how he'll come in, and so forth. While I'm talking, I try to evaluate the hunter as to experience: who's calm and who isn't, who might be able to handle the greatest pressure, and who might be the one to create a problem. Often it's just a feeling I get, but it's very helpful in deciding which hunter to put on which bait. We don't carry backup arms because they aren't legal in Quebec, but my guides carry an ax. In the worst possible case a guide may have to kill a bear with an ax, but that doesn't bother my guides. A bear isn't dangerous until he's closer than three feet, so why be afraid when he's ten feet away? You have to read the bear to see if he's dangerous. You can tell by the way he's acting. If he's not dangerous, you don't need to be armed.

Chapter 3

BAITING GUIDES EVALUATE THE HUNTER

What is your favorite type of hunter (personality, physical abilities, experience level, socioeconomic status, etc.)?

Joe Jakab: I like keen hunters who take a real interest in the wild country we're hunting. I've had great hunts with Europeans who don't even speak English. For example, I had a Czech hunting guide who was here being guided to his own bear. We checked baits together quite a few days and nights before he got his bear. He was a great guy, and I was really happy for him.

Horace Lane: I think my favorite hunter is the guy who doesn't put too much pressure on himself. I like a hunter who comes in with a relaxed attitude that it's not all about the kill: It's more about the experience and seeing the bears out in the wild. The guy who comes in who is interested only in the trophy, and it's got to be the biggest and the best—he's got a problem. Sometimes it's got to be not only the biggest one taken in camp that week but it's got to be the biggest one of the year, or the biggest one ever. That hunter is really putting pressure on himself, and he's setting himself up to go home disappointed. If it's all about the kill the trip is already off to a bad start because we're dealing entirely with free-ranging animals.

You just can't predict what they'll do or whether they'll even come to the bait. The black bear is the cleverest of all the animals in our part of the world; he's totally aware of his surroundings, he's wary, and he may or may not come in. Sometimes he'll even come to the bait when he knows full well that there's a hunter on the stand. He'll play with you, and you need to be ready to play a little with him and not be so serious about how it will all turn out.

Don Lind: My favorite type of hunter is the one who is out for the experience and who feels no pressure to harvest an animal in order to make the hunt a success. Of course, I always hope that the hunter will harvest his trophy, but it takes a lot of pressure off knowing that if things don't work out that way the client will still leave camp satisfied. I don't find that trait to be prevalent in any particular class of people. When it comes to big-game hunts other than bear, I do enjoy hunting with clients that like to get out and hunt hard all day long. That's how I myself hunt, and I enjoy the company of others who like to hunt the same way. Hunters like that appreciate the sights and sounds of the woods. We do not provide a bar service or theater area in our

Hunters come in all sizes, shapes, and abilities. (Photo courtesy of Joe Jakab)

camp, and we don't cater to the hunter who is out for the party more than the hunt.

Claude Turcotte: I like beginners, kids, and women because they will listen to what I tell them. They don't have their own way of doing things, and they do what they are told. I always assume that I'm going to have the worst possible hunter. That's because I want to make certain that we do everything right, and then I can serve that big bear on a silver platter to even the worst hunter. But I do like an experienced hunter with a good personality. Experience in bear hunting really doesn't matter very much to me because my job and my passion are to make it easy for my hunters to harvest the bear they want. I like to guide experienced hunters because with a serious, experienced hunter, I can go for the biggest trophy bears. That kind of hunter will be calm and able to evaluate a bear without seeing the entire animal, and will know a trophy bear at sight and be able to kill it.

Should inexperienced or physically challenged hunters go hunting for black bears? Why or why not?

Joe Jakab: It takes some extra effort on the part of the guides, but I'd say yes, if the inexperienced or physically challenged hunter is keen on the hunt. With such hunters we often put a guide on the stand with them.

Horace Lane: We don't have a problem guiding inexperienced hunters because a lot of our hunters are inexperienced when it comes to hunting black bears. You can do all the reading you want, but until you actually get out and do some hunting, you aren't experienced. Physically challenged hunters, those that can't walk or climb, are really tricky because I like to get my hunters up off the ground for safety reasons. Some hunters, though, even those who aren't handicapped, insist on hunting from the ground, and we allow that. But we usually sit with them just to watch their backside, even though as guides we're not allowed to carry firearms. However, we do usually have licenses for a bear ourselves, and we can be there for the handicapped hunter's protection if that first shot doesn't make a good hit.

It takes a lot of preparation to equip and position a handicapped bow hunter. (Photo courtesy of Claude Turcotte)

Don Lind: I think that a baited black bear hunt is the perfect experience for new bear hunters. Since our hunts are so successful, it gives first-time hunters, using either rifle or bow, the opportunity to harvest their first bear. I think that is very important in this time of diminishing numbers of hunters. A young, first-time hunter that has the enjoyment of harvesting an animal early on will remember the experience forever—and maybe become hooked on hunting! I have encouraged many hunters to bring both bow and rifle on their hunt. A lot of them take their first bear with the rifle, then turn to the bow for the second bear. Some of them have managed to make their first kill ever with the bow, and that gives them confidence in the bow as a weapon. This is also a great experience for hunters with some physical challenge, since a baited bear hunt need not be physically demanding. We have hunted very successfully from ground blinds.

Claude Turcotte: One of my hunters had both legs and one arm paralyzed, and he was shooting a bow with his mouth. Within an hour and a half, we had three bears in front of him, and he got one of them. I was filming him, and he was extremely

Even handicapped hunters can be successful hunting over bait. (Photo courtesy of Claude Turcotte)

calm—maybe because he couldn't run. Obviously, he knew that he had to make a good shot. The bear had actually come up behind him and sniffed at his shoulder, but he couldn't move. It finally circled around him and went to the bait. I don't know what it is, but there is something you give off when you're afraid that makes bears aggressive. If we can keep them calm, the inexperienced and the physically challenged are no problem.

Is there any particular characteristic in hunters that would make you refuse to guide them on a black bear hunt?

Joe Jakab: I would refuse to guide a person who is disrespectful of bears, or who lacks respect after he kills one. You know the type I'm talking about: They walk up to the bear after it's dead and kick it because it's smaller than they'd thought. They won't be back in one of my camps with that attitude.

Horace Lane: I've thought a lot about that question, and I can't think of anything that would make me refuse to guide a person—the first time, that is. There's so much about a person that you can't know beforehand. That's not to say, of course, that they can't do something that would make me refuse them a second hunt—and before the week is out, they'll know they won't be back in my camp again. Attitude problems are the worst. If possible, I take the time to help a hunter amend his attitude if it's all wrong.

Don Lind: I have never yet turned away a client, but I do have one guy in mind that I would refuse to book again. This particular client had never hunted a "wild" animal prior to this hunt. He had hunted only high-fenced game, which I don't have an issue with, but his attitude and expectations were such that he was very demanding of my guides. He literally requested specific bears and suggested that he knew we could provide them and should not hold out till the end of the hunt. He showed no respect for the hard work and efforts of his guides, nor any respect for the animals he was hunting. To him, the bear was just another item for his trophy room. I don't think much of an attitude like that.

Claude Turcotte: I never refuse to guide anyone, but I really don't like it when hunters come into camp thinking that because they paid money they're buying a trophy. Also, I don't like to guide hunters who are overly eager to kill. They give off a different kind of scent to the bear, and even when you put them on the best bait, they will burn it by their very presence. It's not that they move or necessarily do anything wrong, but that they simply ruin the place by what their body releases into the air by their urgency to kill. This happens every year. We always get a hunter like that a bear, but it requires a special effort.

What is the most dangerous thing a client can do while hunting black bears over bait? Can you share an instance in which a client placed himself (or the guide) in danger?

Joe Jakab: Getting lost is probably the most dangerous, although it's also extremely dangerous to run in after a bear immediately after taking a shot at one. I had one hunter shoot at a bear while on the way to the stand. He saw the bear down

A happy hunter with a big bear taken over bait. (Photo courtesy of Claude Turcotte)

a cut line, and, after the shot, he took off after it. Fortunately, I saw it all happen and got there just about the time that the bear charged him in a willow thicket. It was just luck: the hunter killed the bear when it was only ten feet away from him. I say luck because the hunter had his scope turned all the way up to 9X!

Horace Lane: The one thing that comes to mind involves a trio of cubs that came to a bait while a hunter was on stand. He told me that he had actually gotten down off the stand and onto the ground, and that the cubs weren't afraid of him. He had fun getting really close to them.

I asked, "Do you realize what could have happened to you if the mother bear had come in?"

He had no idea what a dangerous situation he had been in. That mother bear could have, and probably would have, been all over him. What a lot of people don't realize about bears, because they look like clumsy, lumbering animals, is how fast they are. In a dash to get back to the tree stand, that guy wouldn't have had a chance.

Don Lind: A couple of things come to mind, the first being that the hunter must always show respect for the black bear. Never take for granted that the bear is afraid of humans. Many of our bears have never had human encounters, and I am totally

Different color phase bears are often taken over bait in the Rocky Mountain West. (Photo courtesy of Don Lind)

convinced that they look at a hunter in a tree stand as a submissive bear that has climbed a tree for safety. Bears are at these baits for the feed. There are frequent battles at these sites for dominance over the food, and the hunter must not be seen as one of the combatants. The hunter must always listen closely to the guide's instructions and take them seriously.

The second point is that we encourage the hunter not to leave the stand until the guide comes by. Again, you don't want to be seen as a rival for the bait, but also, it is very easy to get disoriented or lost when trailing a wounded bear and to discover that you can't get back to the bait site. I always tell hunters that I can't force them to stay in the stand, but if I come in to pick them

Lady hunters can shoot and have success as well as (or better than) the guys! (Photo courtesy of Joe Jakab)

up and they are not there, I couldn't know where to start looking for them in the dark. So I'll go back to camp for supper and a good night's sleep before we start the search the next morning. No one has ever wandered away from the stand!

Claude Turcotte: The danger is relative and related to personal perception. It's rare to have any real danger while hunting black bears. It's more that the darkness seems dangerous. We cover a large area with our hunting, and each guide is picking up four hunters. If two or three have killed a bear, the last guy can be on the stand for an hour after dark, all alone. The bears are very active at that time, and it could be dangerous to come down from the stand and try to walk away from the bait.

Chapter 4

BAITING GUIDES EVALUATE HUNTING ARMS

What is your favorite rifle caliber for black bears, and do you recommend this caliber for clients?

Joe Jakab: There are many good choices, and I don't have a favorite. Any gun that shoots a bullet over 150 grains will work well, although a heavier bullet is better. I like the .30-06, the .35, and the .45-70.

Horace Lane: That question is asked of me quite often, and I don't change the answer for the different animals we hunt. For bears, caribou, or moose, I unequivocally recommend the .30-06. It's my own personal choice, and I find it really effective. I like a wide-angle scope with a big objective that gathers a lot of light at twilight.

We insist that all hunters sight in their rifle on Sunday because we don't hunt on Sunday up here. It gives me a chance to observe how people shoot the bigger calibers. I've told my guides, "If you could film these guys shooting .300 magnums and bigger, you'd see that 90 percent of them close their eyes when they pull the trigger." You can only wonder where the bullet is going to hit after it leaves the barrel.

Don Lind: I think that more important than the caliber is the hunter's ability to know and handle the weapon. A well-placed bullet from any legal caliber (.23 or more) will be effective in putting the bear down. It's obvious, though, that some calibers can help to compensate for a poorly placed shot. One of the best choices I've seen has to be a 12-gauge slug from a rifled shotgun. That weapon is capable of taking out a front shoulder and vitals and still leaving a large exit hole.

Claude Turcotte: I recommend the biggest caliber that the hunter can shoot accurately. Caliber is not important to me.

The bow and arrow is a favorite tool of many hunters when on a baited bear hunt. (Photo courtesy of Don Lind)

I have kids every year with 20-gauge shotguns killing bears. Some guys bring a .243. What I'm more interested in is a low-power scope—no see-through mounts or other gadgets, but a clean, simple gun and scope arrangement. A .30-06 is ideal if the hunter can shoot it well.

If you are on stand with your hunter, what is your choice as a backup weapon when guiding for black bears?

Joe Jakab: As I said before, any gun that shoots a bullet of more than 150 grains is OK, including the .30-06, the .35, and the .45-70.

Horace Lane: In that situation, I'd go with a 12-gauge shotgun with slugs. However, generally we don't carry anything when we go in after a bear because we're not permitted to carry a weapon as a guide. That's the main reason why we usually wait until daylight to follow up the shot. We do always get a bear license ourselves, though, so we can carry protection while we're baiting. We often go in to place bait alone, and we go into areas where we know there are bears active. It's simply prudent to go armed. We try to be brave but not stupid because bears sometimes come in incredibly fast. I've had bears come in within minutes of my putting out the bait, and I've also had them come in and be eating when I return from fetching another bucket.

Don Lind: I personally use either a 12-gauge with alternate loads of slugs and buckshot or a Winchester .375.

Claude Turcotte: In the rare case in which we need a backup weapon, I carry a very short side-by-side 12-gauge shotgun with 00 buckshot. Each pellet is .30 caliber, and in the 3-inch shell there are twelve of them. They're pretty potent at short range. Also, with a double-barrel shotgun you've got two separate trigger mechanisms, so there's no chance of the gun's jamming.

What is your advice on bullet weight? Bullet construction?

Joe Jakab: I have no special recommendations on bullet construction, but a heavier bullet is preferable. I like a bullet that will retain its weight.

Horace Lane: In my favorite rifle, the .30-06, I like a 180-grain bullet, and I recommend the Nosler Partition. I like a bullet that holds its weight on impact, and Noslers are proven performers in the .30-06.

Don Lind: I would recommend using as heavy a bullet as your caliber will permit. I ultimately recommend that my clients always take a broadside shot behind the shoulder, but we don't always get that shot. It's at those times that a well-constructed bullet with some mass will hold together to penetrate bone, take out some vitals, and still leave an exit hole. An exit hole is important for recovering bears that don't drop on the spot. Since most shots

A shotgun that shoots slugs is a good choice when hunting over bait since ranges are usually close. (Photo courtesy of Claude Turcotte)

are from above, a properly placed bullet should leave a low exit wound. That can be critical, since the fat and dense hair covering a bear can plug a small exit hole and make tracking difficult.

I've been really impressed with the Barnes X-Bullet shot from muzzleloaders and slug guns. We have recovered some from bears and found that the bullet has remained largely intact. Also, the butterfly characteristics of the bullet have made excellent wound paths.

Claude Turcotte: I have no special recommendations because I'm not an expert in that field. As I said before, shot placement is much more important than any other factor.

Do you have any tips on shooting techniques in field situations?

Joe Jakab: Have a good scope for shooting in low-light conditions. Bears can come in very late, and on rainy evenings you lose your light fast. Many of our baits are in dark holes, too, and in some places no sunlight even hits the ground. Make certain

In-line muzzleloaders are increasingly popular for taking black bears over bait. (Photo courtesy of Claude Turcotte)

that the scope is turned to the appropriate power, too, and not all the way up to 9X or something.

Horace Lane: Get a rest or use a bipod, if it fits the situation. I'm a good shot, and I can shoot my .30-06 as well as most people, but when possible I always use a rest. It's just prudent.

Don Lind: Since most of our hunting is done from stands, I recommend that clients practice shooting from an elevated, sitting position at close ranges of twenty to twenty-five yards. Not many people practice in these conditions.

Claude Turcotte: Sight in your rifle for thirty to forty yards, maximum. So many experienced hunters come into camp and tell me that for twenty years they've always sighted dead on at two hundred yards, and that puts them four inches high at forty yards. I want it dead on at forty yards. I also like them to shoot groups of less than an inch at forty yards. If they shoot three-inch groups, that causes me to worry, and I tell them to shoot at the body, instead of the shoulder or neck. I tell them to reload and shoot until they have no more bullets in the gun. We show our hunters a video that demonstrates exactly where to aim if the bear is standing broadside, if he's coming toward them, if he's quartering away, and so on.

What advice do you give your hunters regarding shot placement on a black bear?

Joe Jakab: Shoot behind the shoulder, or if you're shooting a really heavy bullet of 180 to 220 grains, you can place it through the shoulder, which is my personal favorite shot. Always shoot your bear twice if you have the chance. If you flip the bear with the shot, you probably hit him high in the shoulder, and he can be on his feet and gone in seconds. That has happened many times, so just make up your mind to put that second shot in as quickly as you can get it off. Forget about head shots.

Horace Lane: I always recommend the heart-lung vital area placement. I don't want the hunter to try to break the near shoulder with the shot because the bullet might contact enough bone that it doesn't reach the vitals. A bear can go a long way if you don't get the bullet into the chest. It's OK to try to break the opposite shoulder after the bullet has passed through the heart-lung area, but I recommend against trying to break the shoulder that's facing you.

Don Lind: I always encourage any big-game hunter to make a broadside shot just behind the shoulder, and midway through the body vertically on all animals. I think that's important because it presents the biggest target and will ultimately take down the animal. We can always track down a fatally wounded animal, but if you misplace a shoulder, neck, or head shot, the wounded animal may never be found. If your target presents a slightly angled shot where you can take out a front shoulder as well, that is acceptable because your main target is still the heart-lung area. I don't like the idea of taking out the front shoulders of any animal to "take them down." If the shot is just slightly forward of the intended target area, you may have a brisket shot that skims in front of the vitals, and then you've got an animal that you won't recover. In our camp, a wounded animal is considered a dead animal, so make sure that shot counts.

Claude Turcotte: We advise our hunters to shoot at the base of the neck, near where the shoulder joins the body. Such a shot drops the bear on the spot. Some people start to get nervous when a really big bear comes in. They are tempted to go for the body, and that's where the trouble arises. If you're shooting a big caliber, try to put it through both shoulders, reload, and shoot again. With a bow, I have hunters place the arrow behind the shoulder.

How many of your first-time black bear hunters are intimidated by the prospect of hunting a dangerous animal? Describe some typical reactions.

Joe Jakab: First-time hunters can certainly be a little worried. The woods are big, and the hunter is alone and a long way from people. Hunters may want to come out way too early. In Quebec and Ontario, we can legally hunt until a half-hour past sunset, and at the forty-eighth parallel it stays light until 9:30 or 10:30 P.M. in May and June. On a rainy evening it gets dark early, and some guys get spooked.

In Quebec, guns have to be cased after legal shooting hours. One time a conservation officer drove up to one of our hunters, who was standing along the road with a rifle in his hands, well past legal shooting hours.

The officer asked if the gun was loaded, and the hunter said, "Yes, officer, it's loaded, and my guide told me the gun should be cased. I'll just take the ticket and keep my gun loaded and ready until I get picked up!" I drove up about that time, and the officer just smiled and let it go.

Horace Lane: I think part of the appeal of bear hunting is the rush of excitement you get from hunting something that can bite you, and something of which you have a natural fear. I don't see it as a real problem for most hunters. That's why they're here, for the excitement.

Don Lind: A couple of our clients each year are somewhat apprehensive about hunting something that might hunt or eat them. We spend some time with all our clients the first day going over "Bear Hunting 101" in order to prepare them for their hunt. Usually after the first night or two everyone settles in and enjoys the hunt. We have had some requests that we sit with hunters at the bait sites, and also requests to have some clients out of the bush before dark. I really appreciate the hunter who has the honesty to say that he's scared of being in the dark with a bunch of bears under his stand. No one needs to experience such fright to the extent that it lessens the enjoyment of the hunt.

Claude Turcotte: There's a pretty high percentage that are at least a little apprehensive. "Scared" may be too strong a word, but a few will admit that they're actually afraid.

How do you prepare for and handle overpowering excitement in clients?

Joe Jakab: I've sat with young lads who just shook like crazy when a bear approached. It's pretty common to get excited, especially when a person is inexperienced. I have those hunters simply close their eyes until they regain their composure. I've even advised hunters, if they're sitting alone, to let a bear go if they can't make a confident, relaxed shot. It's far better for the bear to leave unmolested than for the hunter to take a shot without being composed.

Horace Lane: Preparation is critical since the problem doesn't occur until the animal is right in front of them. You've got to talk to them a little ahead of time, telling them again all the things they've known all their lives: what to expect, how they might feel, and how the bear might present. I have them relax so as to make sure of their shot, and just talk to them thoroughly.

Don Lind: Again, we do our "Bear Hunting 101" with all hunters, so that they have some insight into what might happen on the hunt. Another thing I do is not to downplay the excitement or anticipation, but try to answer any and all questions honestly. I think that the excitement and anticipation are very important to the enjoyment of the hunt.

Claude Turcotte: The best way to counter it is to see a lot of animals. Many times if I'm concerned about a person, I go and sit with him on the stand. I take the hunter to an active bait

This happy hunter used her stainless steel shotgun to take a fine bruin over bait. (Photo courtesy of Joe Jakab)

and let him look at a lot of bears. If the big one comes in, it's over. You look at my pictures, and you'll see that all the kids have a really nice, big bear.

Do you have any wise words on bowhunting? Black-powder hunting?

Joe Jakab: Bow hunters should let the bear relax at the bait. When the bear first arrives it can be very nervous, and it's difficult to draw a bow without being noticed. After the bear eats a bit it will relax considerably. Bears will often take bits of bait and walk off a distance to eat. They have incredible hearing, so your clothing must be quiet, as must your bow rest. For bow hunters, broadside shots behind the shoulder are good, but quartering shots going away are even better. When looking at the bear, your arrow trajectory should be such that it exits at the bear's opposite front knee. Black-powder hunters should wait for a broadside shot, and after the shot they should listen before reloading: You may hear the telltale repetitive moans that mean a dead bear. If you missed, just sit tight. For some reason bears (and other game) don't seem to fear the roar of a muzzleloader; they will often return fairly soon, or even just stand there without leaving.

Horace Lane: We do take both types of hunters. Particularly with bow hunters, we have a hard time getting some of them to take a firearm to the stand with them. A true bow hunter has a resistance to having a firearm along, and can I understand that. But my wise word is to take a shotgun for use if you're in danger. If that bear starts coming up the ladder, there's nothing to shoot at with a bow, but with a shotgun you've got protection. I recommend that the bow hunter take to the stand a 12-gauge shotgun with slugs as a backup. A bear you can't stop can do a lot of damage in a short time, and it's smart to have that shotgun with you, in my opinion. It's perfectly all right to have any legal firearm on the stand with you in Newfoundland. The main thing about black-powder hunting is that, like bowhunting, it means only one shot. You need either to be able to reload really quickly, or to have that shotgun with you as a backup.

Don Lind: Being an avid bow hunter and muzzleloader hunter, I have a lot to say on this topic. I know that there are outfitters who think these weapons have no place in their camps, but I totally disagree. I just emphasize that the hunter must be competent with these weapons, which are very effective when used properly.

The bow is a very lethal weapon in the hands of a responsible hunter. I again go back to the importance of shot placement. I will also contradict many outfitters with the comment that I believe that mechanical broadheads are an excellent choice for bear hunting. The flight of most mechanicals is identical to that of target points, and, since most bow hunters shoot target points 95 percent of the time, that is important. The biggest reason I like

Tyler Lind, son of outfitter Don Lind, used a bow to take his first bear. (Photo courtesy of Don Lind)

mechanicals, though, is that most will provide a large-diameter exit wound unrivaled my most fixed-blade broadheads.

As I mentioned earlier, the bigger exit wound makes tracking easier. Bears are a thin-skinned animal, so hide penetration is not an issue. A well-placed shot into the lung area from a bow or muzzleloader is very effective. I know, for example, that we have lost fewer animals shot by bow, muzzleloader, and shotgun hunters than by centerfire rifle hunters. That is because the bow or muzzleloader hunter is used to having to be patient and wait for the perfect shot. Too many rifle hunters attempt bad shots, thinking that they can make it, or that their weapon will make that low-percentage shot for them. Shot placement is always the most important factor in humanely harvesting an animal.

Claude Turcotte: Some years 30 percent of my hunters are bow hunters, and I have a lot of black-powder hunters. I also push the shotgun because I like it very much for bears. I really don't mind taking bow hunters, but I don't like it when hunters show up with both a bow and a gun because that means they're not good, serious bow hunters. They want to use the bow for a few days and then switch to the rifle. It's best to specialize in one or the other, but not both. With black powder I want a neck shot because there's no second chance; I want them to drop the bear in its tracks. I've never really had a bad experience with muzzleloader hunters.

Do you take any special precautions when hunting with bow hunters or black-powder hunters?

Joe Jakab: I tell them to make the first shot count.

Horace Lane: Having a shotgun on the stand would be my recommended special precaution for those hunters.

Don Lind: Since all of our bait sites are set up for twenty- to twenty-five-yard shots, all the sites are suitable for all the hunters that visit our camp. Our sites are also far enough apart that a rifle hunter shooting at one site will have no effect on the bow hunter at the next. I don't take any special precautions with bow or muzzleloader hunters other than re-emphasizing the importance of the perfect shot.

Claude Turcotte: If they bring both a bow and a gun, I tell them to take the gun. If they're serious about bowhunting, they'll kill the bear with the bow.

Chapter 5

HUNTING BLACK BEARS OVER BAIT

What is the most common mistake made by guided black bear hunters?

Joe Jakab: Shooting too quickly is the most common mistake. They tend not to let a spooky bear come in to the bait so that they can carefully look him over. When they rush to shoot, it greatly increases their odds of shooting a young bear, which is another common mistake.

Horace Lane: I think it's the desire to stay too late on the stand, and be on the stand when the light has failed to the point that it's no longer safe to shoot. We tell people that a two-hundred-pound black bear also has two hundred pounds of shadow just at dark, and that's when it's really easy to make a major mistake in shot placement. Anything black gets even blacker as the light fails, and you really can't place a shot properly if your target looks twice as big as it really is. Generally we go in and retrieve the hunter when darkness begins to fall, but some guys complain about our coming too early. Our hunters also have radios and can tell us if they're ready to come out.

Don Lind: I'd say that the most common mistake—if you want to call it that—is assuming that you should not shoot the first bear you see. Often hunters have gone into the stand with that idea and have videoed some better than average bears. One of the better bears taken in our camp was a Boone and Crockett boar taken fifteen minutes after the hunter was placed in the stand his first night out.

On the other hand, I do get a lot of hunters who have hunted other areas without spotting a single bear, so they shoot the first one they see, regardless of size. Each season we will have one or two hunters who will harvest both of their bears the first

There's a big one in the area! (Photo courtesy of Joe Jakab)

night out. When the hunter tags out, we don't haul him off to the airport or kick him out of camp. We expect the successful hunter to enjoy the rest of his stay and the hunting adventures of the other camp members.

Claude Turcotte: Shooting too quickly and not waiting for the right bear is very common. I don't get upset when they tell me that they've passed up four or five bears because they're waiting for the big one. I'll move them around until I show them the right one; they don't need to shoot the first bear they see.

What can guided hunters do that would most improve their chances of taking their game (for example, patience, physical fitness, mental preparation, equipment, practice with choice of weapon)?

Joe Jakab: Patience is most important because hunting bears over bait is a waiting game. You've got to be prepared for long waits amid swarms of insects that want to eat you alive. The hunter's odds are greatly improved if he uses a modern firearm. I'm a bow hunter and have taken several Pope and Young bears, but there are some bears that can be extremely difficult to take with a bow.

Horace Lane: I'd put at the top of the list patience, plus some mental preparation. All hunters should practice with their weapon, too, of course, and they should practice shooting from an elevation, which does change the bullet or arrow impact point.

Don Lind: The hunter must be prepared to spend 6 to 8 hours on the stand each afternoon. That requires a lot of patience, especially for hunters who haven't done much stand hunting. The hunter has to be confident and skilled with his weapon and be practiced at shooting from a seated, elevated position at close range.

Claude Turcotte: Finding the right outfitter with the right territory is the most important thing they can do. After that, they need to listen to the guide and do what he says. Never try your own little tricks, like putting out some kind of scent, because a strange smell can ruin the bait.

Besides the weapon, what kind of equipment should every hunter carry? Also, what is the most important single piece of equipment?

Joe Jakab: Binoculars are pretty handy, even though you're set up close to the bait. A good flashlight is also important.

Horace Lane: Something for safety is important, such as pepper spray. You might encounter an aggressive animal that tries to climb in the stand with you, or one that you simply want to move out of there but don't want to kill. The pepper spray is a good precaution.

Don Lind: I would have to say that the single most important piece of equipment would likely be a safety harness. I used to provide safety harnesses, but hunters either took them home with them at the end of the hunt or left them in the stands, where the bears destroyed them. Also, some hunters prefer specific types of harnesses. Safety in stands is the number one concern.

Secondly, hunters should always be prepared to spend a night in the woods. We are hunting true wilderness, and anything can happen. I assure hunters that we will get them out, but sometimes things occur that dictate a late evening in the stand. Hunters should pack a flashlight, fire starter, and warm clothing, just in case.

Claude Turcotte: For the gun hunter, shooting sticks are a big help. For bow hunters, it's important to have a good bow sling to pull the bow up. If you're hunting alone, which our hunters don't normally do, a compass and knife are important. Our hunters don't even take a flashlight because if they use it on the bait they can ruin it.

Are there any common items of equipment that you feel are unnecessary, redundant, or just plain worthless for hunting black bears over bait?

Joe Jakab: Most hunters tend to load up a pack with far more gear than they need. You want to travel light, so you can slip in and out of your stand quietly; you don't need to be fishing around in a bag full of gadgets. When you leave your stand, it's equally important to be stealthy because there's a high probability that a bear is nearby. We almost always walk in and escort our hunters from the stand, but still it's important that the hunter be able to get in and out quietly.

Noel Weigel took his first black bear with a bow. (Photo courtesy of Noel Weigel)

Horace Lane: While you're on a baited stand, there's an awful lot of equipment you really don't need—such as binoculars, fire starter, and the like. You're in radio contact and just don't need those things. They're not worthless, but they are of limited value in our situation. I send out a list of items labeled "must have" and "nice to have," and that tends to keep down the amount of worthless gear our hunters bring in.

Don Lind: I find that more and more hunters pack too much equipment with them; after the first night they sort through their packs and minimize their gear. Although binoculars are nice, if the hunter follows instructions the bears will be within twenty to twenty-five yards, so binoculars are pretty much

A big hide taken by a happy hunter. (Photo courtesy of Joe Jakab)

unnecessary. Also, many hunters bring an attractant scent that they're convinced will call in the big one. We use specific scents at our sites, and I believe that a foreign scent would alert some bears to a change in the routine. In our area there is no requirement for particular colors of clothing, so I recommend a wardrobe of your favorite brand of camouflage in a boreal forest color or pattern.

Claude Turcotte: The worst thing they can bring with them is a big backpack full of all kinds of junk. They can't get to the stand quietly with the pack on, and when they're on the stand they're moving around, zipping and unzipping and rustling around inside, giving away the fact that they're there. When a hunter comes to camp with an attachment to a big pack, I know I've got trouble.

Tell us your method of field judging black bears for size. How do you present this to clients before they go to the stand?

Joe Jakab: Bears that are especially big have a dent in their forehead about the size of an ashtray. Big bears also appear to have small ears, short snouts, and rounded features. Big and older bears move with slow deliberation, while young bears are nervous and jerky in their movements. We have some mounted bears in the lodge, and we discuss size, as well as shot placement, using those mounts. We use white five-gallon buckets wired to trees as bait containers. These containers are 16 inches high, and a big bear on all fours stands about 34 inches high. A really good bear is 5½ to 6 feet in length and weighs some 250 to 350 pounds. The depth of the chest on a bear that big would be some 4 inches higher than the top of the bucket. Also, a large bear cannot get his head into one of those buckets. We teach our hunters how to put all of these factors together when judging big bears.

Horace Lane: We have a full mount black bear in the camp, and we give our hunters some idea from that. We always tell them to look at the size of the ears compared with the head. We tell them that if it looks like a German shepherd, it's probably not much bigger than a German shepherd. As the ears get smaller, the bear is generally bigger. We also use the rings on the fifty-five-gallon drums that we use for baiting. If the bear is only up to the first ring, it's a small bear. If it's up to the second ring, it's a medium-size bear, and if it's up to the top of the barrel, shoot right away!

Father and son together on stand. (Photo courtesy of Claude Turcotte)

Don Lind: Most of our sites are equipped with a fifty-five-gallon drum for bait storage. That can be used as an indicator of size. A bear that stands two-thirds of the way up the barrel is an average bear, about 5½ feet squared. A bear that stands on all fours with its back at the same height or over the top of the barrel is above average and will square 6½ to 7 feet.

I also tell hunters that an immature bear is built somewhat like a German shepherd dog. If the bear's nose is long and its ears look long and pointed, and if it looks like it has long legs with plenty of air space between its belly and the ground, it is an immature bear. Also, a mature bear should have about three ear widths between the inside base of the ears, and its ears will look shorter and rounded, not pointed. The apparent lack of a neck is also a sign of a mature, muscled-up bear. A mature boar will develop a crease in its forehead that runs parallel with the nose.

Yet another indicator may be the bear's disposition at the bait site. Younger bears are generally timid and spend a lot of time looking over their shoulder in case the big guy is coming in. A mature bear often rules the site, and his disposition will show his dominance. All of these indicators must be noted to assist in the judging of a potential trophy. I have read, and I truly believe, that a bear is the most difficult animal to judge for trophy quality. It is also important to realize that bears have individual traits. We have taken some mature boars with nineteen- to twenty-inch skulls that were long-legged, big-eared males.

Claude Turcotte: When a big bear is present, you just seem to feel its presence. When you see the bear's head, you can usually tell by looking at the forehead, where there are two big muscles that you can see, and they're separated significantly on a big bear. The bait barrel is a fifty-five-gallon drum, and it has two rings separating it into thirds. I tell my hunters never to shoot a bear unless it's more than halfway to the top above the second ring—a big bear is almost as tall as the barrel. If the hunter is experienced, I tell him not to shoot unless the bear is taller than the barrel. In front of the barrel are two white buckets, and a big bear has a head that will hardly fit inside.

What is the most reliable way to determine sex when no cubs are present? Give us some other methods as well.

Joe Jakab: Cubs will generally come in with their mother to the bait, but, rarely, they will come in up to five minutes later. That can cause a problem, but because we prebait months ahead, I generally know what kinds of bears are about. Cubs leave a lot of sign—scratching on trees and lots of small droppings. We keep on baiting such sites, but we don't hunt them. Avoiding such sites is the best way to keep from shooting a female.

Horace Lane: I can almost always tell a male from a female by the length of the snout, even in a mounted bear. I don't know how scientifically reliable this is, but it seems to work. Bears are the most difficult of animals we hunt to sex, so we rely heavily on facial features. The males generally have a shorter, wider, and thicker snout.

Don Lind: I believe that not even the most experienced bear hunter can always tell a sow from a boar. If you happen to have two mature bears at a site, likely one of them is a male—or both may be sows, as two mature males rarely get along. I can often discern a sow from a boar by the facial features. Females will not acquire the large head of a mature boar, and will show somewhat more feminine features; also, they rarely have the crease in the forehead caused by the muscle buildup of mature boars. A very mature sow will have a low-hanging midbelly area, but I think that is only evident in the older sows. It's very difficult to differentiate between a middle-aged boar and an older sow without the presence of cubs.

Claude Turcotte: It's mostly a question of size, though it's very possible to determine sex by body characteristics. The female is shorter and stockier than the male. That's difficult for the inexperienced bear hunter to judge, though. The best cue is size because very few female bears will be as tall as two-and-a-half rings on the bait barrel. Also, the hair is much finer on a sow, and much longer, especially on the neck. It's almost like a mane.

How do you normally proceed to follow up after a shot at a black bear?

Joe Jakab: We provide our hunters with radios, and they are instructed to radio us thirty minutes after the shot.

Making a video of the hunt is fun, but it takes a lot more work. (Photo courtesy of Claude Turcotte)

Sometimes we have remaining light, and sometimes we don't. I like for the hunter to remain in the stand and then walk me directly to where the bear was standing—but I can tell you, a lot of hunters can sure misdirect you! I then try to determine how hard the bear is hit.

Horace Lane: The first thing to do as a hunter is to stop and listen. Bears give off an eerie death moan that's very characteristic. If you hear it, you need to mark the location carefully. Then the hunter waits for the guide to arrive before getting down, and the two of them will go and check the area. Failing to find the bear, if it is getting dark they will return the next morning and begin an intensive search.

Tracking a bear in thick cover comes with the territory. (Photo courtesy of Claude Turcotte)

Don Lind: The first thing is to ask the hunter his thoughts on the shot. That is usually a good indication on what can be expected in retrieving a downed bear. Sometimes, if there is uncertainty with shot placement, we can be in for a long tracking job. Secondly, we ask the hunter what the bear's reactions were after the shot, which direction it was headed in, where it was last seen, what the bear was doing when it was last seen, and so forth.

Claude Turcotte: If the hunter shoots and the bear doesn't drop in its tracks, I have the hunter mark the exit trail the bear took. In order to track that bear, we need to see blood. There are so many trails behind the bait that they're like highways, and we must know where to start. I tell the hunter never to get down from the stand because there could be a lot of danger—not from the bear he's shot but from another one. Maybe he shot the sow that a big male was following, she's dead thirty yards away, and the big guy is coming in. The hunter is in big trouble if he's down. He's got to stay on the stand until we come.

What procedure do you follow in tracking a wounded black bear?

Joe Jakab: If I believe that the bear could still be alive, I wait until morning to follow the trail. Otherwise, we follow the track immediately. We have no exemptions permitting us to carry a firearm or any weapon after legal hours, so we do a lot of tracking and recovery unarmed after dark.

Horace Lane: When you're following a track, you take something white with you to mark any blood trail you find. It's necessary to do that because it's amazing how much red there is in the ground carpet here in Newfoundland. It looks like there's no red at all until you start looking for a blood trail, and then there's red everywhere. But we meticulously follow until there's nothing left to give us clues, or until we find the bear.

Don Lind: If we are confident that the hunter has made a well-placed shot and we can locate the bear readily, we will take up the trail. If we have any doubts about a quick recovery, we get the assistance of another guide before taking up the trail.

Claude Turcotte: We've got to find blood in order to follow the bear, but we don't need much. Bears usually don't bleed much. Bears don't stop like deer. They keep going until they die, so you have to stay on the track until you find them. We may find only a spot of blood every ten feet, but that's enough if the shot was sufficient to kill the bear.

Chapter 6

SPECIFIC GUIDING AREAS FOR HUNTING OVER BAIT

Describe your home guiding area for black bears, and any distinctions that set it apart.

Joe Jakab: We hunt in the Domaine Forsythe, an area owned by Jean Leo and Gemma Berbube. It's located forty miles east of Sennetere, Quebec, Canada. Domaine Forsythe is located on the only east-west forestry road in a huge wilderness. We have no other outfitters bordering us on three sides, so there are huge bear reservoirs all around us.

Horace Lane: We don't have a lot of elevation here, with our highest terrain being about fifteen hundred feet. There are a lot of steep but low hills scattered throughout our area, and on those hills there are a lot of berries. Bears spend a lot of time there in the fall. I think that they end up hibernating in the areas where they feed extensively in the fall, and you see them there in the spring. We have a lot of those little rolling hills with outcroppings of rock, and it's really good black bear habitat. Because of our one thousand miles of forest access road, the land is fairly accessible, so we can get in to set out our baits and get our stands in place.

Don Lind: There is a mix of densely forested Crown (state) land and privately held agricultural area within our unit's boundaries. The core of tree-covered land and a fringe area of agricultural land makes ideal habitat for the area's wildlife. The river systems and forested lands provide safety, and the agricultural lands offer an abundance of feed for wildlife. We have many bears that prefer the denser woods for safety but rely on the grains and crops as a valuable food source.

Claude Turcotte: We have some hills and a dense mixed conifer and hardwood forest. I have exclusive rights to hunt two provincial hunting areas, Mastiguouche and Ste-Maurice wildlife preserves. The first is 975 square miles, and the other is more than four hundred square miles. There is also a piece of land between the preserves that's some seven hundred square miles. Nobody can hunt there but my hunters. Out of that vast area we take only about thirty bears per year, and that's why we have so many huge bears: The hunting pressure is light. It's also why we can offer each hunter a virgin bait because the area is so large. I have about sixty bait stations in that whole area, and they're so widely spread that it takes us three days to bait them all.

What kind of area is ideal for hunting black bears over bait?

Joe Jakab: A really good area has a high "Habitat Stability Index," a term that biologists use to indicate a mixed, mature, unbroken forest. Mixed forests of poplar, birch, and maple are where bears find their most reliable food sources. There is active new growth in spring, including ferns, shoots of all sorts, bud ends, and other highly concentrated energy sources. After the spring explosion of growth, insects become a major protein source. Spruce and pine provide excellent cover but very little food production. If I'm flying over or driving through an area, any ridgeline covered with poplars and aspens running through a large tamarack swamp would look like a prime baiting site. If that ridgeline happened to have a spring near the top, you have found an excellent spot. Bottlenecks are easy to find, such as a point between two lakes, and those are also good places to establish feeding stations.

Horace Lane: You've got to find areas where a bear feels safe coming to a bait because he's got good cover nearby. We don't put our baits out in big, wide-open areas because the bears are reluctant to come to them. We find a small area that's fairly open but has lots of cover on approaches to the bait. There are areas that have low balsam fir that are ideal. We put our stands on nearby larger trees, and it really works for us.

A classic bear camp in springtime. (Photo courtesy of Noel Weigel)

Don Lind: I like to find a place with dense, heavy cover away from high-traffic areas and usually along heights of ground or watercourses.

Claude Turcotte: It needs to have water because bears are very thirsty in the spring. We hunt close to creeks, but far enough away that you can't hear the water, the noise of which makes bears spooky. Bears like it when there are willows and poplar because they like to eat the leaves. They also like grass, which they need to clean the stomach in the spring.

Describe your typical camp setup and camp routine.

Joe Jakab: Domaine Forsythe has several cabins and apartment-type rooms in the main lodge. My guides and I begin baiting in the morning and return to get the hunters out at about 3:00 P.M., depending on logistics. We generally have three hunters per guide. The guides and hunters all have lunch together, and we discuss strategy for the evening. Hunters are welcome to participate in the baiting, too.

Horace Lane: We've got a comfortable lodge with three bedrooms and three baths, and we have a full-time cook and all the amenities. The cook is up early getting breakfast ready by 6:30 or 7:00 A.M., and the guides leave to put out new bait. The hunter has the option of going with them, or he can stay around camp and relax until they get back. Then it's a matter of choosing which bait to sit over that evening, and it may or may not be the one he was on the night before, depending on what happens as the guides put out more bait. Quite often, though, a hunter on a good bait is perfectly willing to spend his five nights of hunting there because he knows there's a good bear in the area.

Don Lind: Our bear camp is located on acreage within the hunting area. We have a serviced location with power and water facilities. Our sleeping unit is a kind of trailer that is built like a mobile home. It has four individual bedrooms with wooden framed beds and standard mattresses. We accommodate two hunters per room under normal circumstances. The sleeping unit is heated with a forced air, propane fueled furnace. Our washhouse is a wooden frame building with a flush toilet, shower, and wash sink with a hot and cold pressurized system. Our kitchen unit is currently a 14- by 16-foot canvas tent on a wooden frame and floor. The kitchen unit has wood heating, a microwave, propane stove, electric refrigerator, and even a television.

A typical day often starts with a photo session of the previous day's trophies. We usually have breakfast around 9:00 A.M., and then we skin or cape the hunters' harvest. We prefer to freeze the hides for shipment home with the hunters, or else send them to a local taxidermist. Since 11 September 2001, airlines have been refusing to accept any package containing salt products. If hunters want to take any bear meat home with them (not required by Alberta law), the animal will be prepared the night the bear is harvested and the meat frozen.

After the bears from the day before are ready, the guides start preparing the bait for the day's runs. Hunters may take

Accommodations for baited hunts can be rustic or plush. (Photo courtesy of Claude Turcotte)

this time to assist the guides, do some target shooting, or maybe just catch a nap. We have a large lunch around 1:00 P.M., and about 3:00 P.M. we start out for the afternoon hunt. Each guide takes a maximum of two hunters.

We do not assign hunters to a particular guide for the entire week. I like to swap hunters and hunting areas around, so that everyone gets a full experience. When the hunters are placed at their respective hunting sites, the guides go to check their assigned baits. We pick up the first hunter shortly after legal shooting time is over, a half-hour after sunset, and then the second hunter as soon as possible after the first. When we return to camp we have a hot meal and turn in for the day.

Claude Turcotte: The place we hunt used to be a private hunting area for very rich Americans. We use the cabin they built, which is old but very nice. We hunt only in the afternoon. If we've killed bears the night before, we may not get through skinning them until early afternoon. We have lunch around 2:00 or 3:00 P.M., and we leave between then and 5:00, depending on the weather and how far the bait is from camp. If it's bad weather, I hold the hunters in camp longer. We hunt until almost 10:00 P.M., and we're back in camp by midnight for supper and in bed by 1:00 A.M. That schedule makes it almost impossible to hunt in the mornings, or everybody gets burned out. But it's not necessary to hunt in the mornings.

Describe your typical stand setup for hunting black bears over bait.

Joe Jakab: Our stands are set in mature forests in or near pine and spruce cover. Stands and baits are, on average, two to five hundred yards into the timber. Stands vary from twelve to fifty yards from the bait, the closer distances being for bow hunters and the longer ones for rifle hunters. Most of the stands are twelve to sixteen feet in height, and all rifle stands have rifle rests. Most stands are metal ladder stands, and are portable. I have about fifty such stands. The setups are located in such an area and at such a distance that a bear can't completely circle the bait without feeling restricted by a road or a large clearing. It is important that the bear be comfortable about approaching the bait. If the bear is comfortable, he will come in much earlier than if he is not.

Horace Lane: We use wooden platforms built in between three or four fairly good trees. Our trees in Newfoundland aren't all that big, so we position our stands in between several. Each one has a wooden ladder leading up to the platform. We generally enclose the platform with fresh boughs, so there's a natural kind of camouflage in place. We also put a rail around the whole thing, too, for safety, as well as a place to rest the rifle. Our stands are built big enough for two people, and we make them comfortable by putting in some kind of seat.

Don Lind: All of our sites have ladder-type stands. I have found these to be the most comfortable and safest. Stand heights are typically sixteen feet or so, with the bait barrel placed about twenty to twenty-five yards in front of the stand location. The access hole in the bait barrel is small, so the bears have to work and concentrate on the task at hand.

A good camp has a clean, well-staffed kitchen. (Photo courtesy of Claude Turcotte)

The purpose for this is twofold: First, it ensures that the bait will not be quickly consumed by the first bears to arrive. Second, with the bears focusing on their food source, hunters have an outstanding opportunity to position themselves for a shot without being detected.

Claude Turcotte: Before I put out a bait, I have a list of things that must be present to make it appropriate. We look for water, the right vegetation, good truck access for baiting, and so on. We use the elevation and the dominant wind direction to position the stand or ground blind. We use mostly portable ladder stands with a good shooting rail for a rest. We want an elevation to the east where we can put the stand, with the bait to the west. If all of my conditions aren't met, I don't put a bait there. When we're baiting, we do all the things we don't want the hunter to do—we make noise, we spread our scent around, we talk loudly, and we let the guide smoke if he's a smoker. We even tie a piece of sweaty clothing on a tree near the bait and spray it with musk oil. We get in and do all of this in five minutes or less because if we stay too long, we might cause a bear to leave, particularly a big one. We do it to condition the bear to being baited.

We have two trails going to the bait site, one going to the tree stand and one going to the bait. When it's time for the hunter to go in, he sneaks in without any noise at all. We put the hunter up quietly and put our bait out with the usual noise and get out of there quickly. The bear thinks it's lunch as usual if we do it right. Very often the hunter kills the bear before the guides get back to the main trail, in less than five minutes. It happened that way about a third of the time this year.

What kind of bait do you use, and how do you go about using it to attract black bears?

Joe Jakab: I run seventy baits for forty hunters in an area of more than six hundred square miles. We have over two hundred road miles to run in putting out our baits, and the baits are a minimum of four miles apart. That helps to reduce the problem of a bear using more than one bait site. I use ten tons of crushed cookies, four fifty-five-gallon drums of frying grease, and six tons of meat from local butchers. We start with a base of cookies and grease, but the prime bait is meat. Older bears definitely prefer meat.

Horace Lane: We use all the trimmings we can get from the local butchers. We depend on meat heavily in the early spring because bears use their sense of smell to locate food sources. They also need some green in their gut, and we have a lot of aspen, birch, maple, and grasses that fill that need. These are close to our baits, too. After they start hitting the baits, we keep them coming with bakery sweets, such as day-old bread mixed with molasses, which the bears love. We do tend to mix up their diet as time goes by, just to keep them interested.

Don Lind: We have used bakery products such as discarded breads, pastries, and bulk cookies. I have also used oats,

A young hunter with a big bear—and he killed an animal, too! (Photo courtesy of Claude Turcotte)

molasses, bulk dry dog food, beaver carcasses, and meat by-products from local abattoirs. I used to think, and many outfitters still do think, that you must have plenty of meat or beaver scraps and carcasses to be a successful bear guide or hunter. Our experience over the past several years has proven that false. In the past two years I have used a combination of baits, including no meat by-products at all, and there has been no change in the number or size of bears that we have taken. Again, I think that a substantial food source is more important than a specific food type. What's most important is to get the bears to the bait site for the first time. Bears have an excellent sense of smell and can apparently smell fresh blood for up to two miles under ideal conditions. Without giving away all of my secrets, I'll say that I have developed a few attractant scents and scenting methods that seem to work very well. These scents get the bait sites started, and then the bears work at spreading the scents through their normal travel and at their bedding areas. That attracts more bears. Since we use such a volume of bait, acquiring a particular source year after year can be a challenge.

Claude Turcotte: We start baiting a month before the hunters come. The main bait we use to attract big bears is fresh meat, which we put out twice a week. I have a connection to a slaughterhouse operation, and we put out forty thousand pounds of meat a year. On my best baits I sometimes put up to one thousand pounds of fresh meat, with less on secondary baits. Most outfitters can't get meat in such quantity, so they use other things, like cake. After the bears start coming to a bait, you can begin using other stuff, such as bread, grain, French fries, and so forth, but it takes fresh meat to get them started.

I've got my own ideas about how to set up a bait in order to attract the most bears—and also the biggest. You can set out a bait and attract bear because they're just like a big raccoon. What's hard is to take the big ones consistently. Sometimes a bait isn't working; you move it one thousand feet, or even less, and all of a sudden where there were no bears there are suddenly ten or more. And then sometimes the bears won't come in when you put a hunter on the stand. So you move the bait fifty yards, and you're often successful. It's a big, complicated game, but we play it well by fine-tuning our baits.

What is your success rate on trophy animals?

Joe Jakab: We are allocated forty-one licenses for bear, and we generally have 93 to 97 percent success filling our tags. The average spring bear we take is six years old and weighs about 180 pounds. That is much larger than the provincial average. About 25 percent of our hunters will take bears in the eight-to-twelve-year-old class, and those bears weigh 250 to 350 pounds. These sizes are not exaggerated in the least, but I must warn you, estimates from many outfits are often greatly overblown.

Horace Lane: We have about 10 to 20 percent that will make Boone and Crockett skull sizes of twenty to twenty-one inches. We're taking bears that weigh three hundred pounds or more, but not all of them have skull sizes in the true trophy range close to twenty-one inches. Of course, the trophy is in the eye of the beholder, and many people are extremely happy with a big-bodied bear, regardless of how well the skull scores. Opportunities at a decent bear are in the range of 100 percent.

Don Lind: The success rate on trophy animals varies annually, depending on what standards you use and the group of hunters that come through camp. Typically we will get one or two bears each year that will be very near or meet the Boone and Crockett minimum of a twenty-one-inch skull. We will also get five or six that meet the eighteen-inch Pope and Young minimum. If the majority of hunters through camp are first-time bear hunters, trophy statistics are lower, since many will take the first average-size bear they see. Our success rate on colored bears is also very good. Annually, 30 to 40 percent of the bears harvested in our camp are a color phase other than black. Again, the success rate varies annually, depending on the hunters' selections. In one recent spring, 60 percent of the bears harvested at the end of week three were a color phase other than black.

Thick woods hide this hunter and blind. (Photo courtesy of Claude Turcotte)

Claude Turcotte: I guarantee a kill. My success rate is 100 percent, and most of them are big bears.

Describe your usual hunting method and any common variations.

Joe Jakab: Since we begin baiting a month before our hunters start to arrive, some bears catch onto what we are doing and will be waiting for the bait to be dropped off. The bears are still wary but will come in rather quickly after the truck's departure. We try to walk our hunters in, and we've had some quick kills almost on the heels of the departing guide. We also walk in to retrieve most hunters, in order to create an outside disturbance and push off any nearby circling bear. We have also dropped hunters on baits early if we suspect that a bear is waiting for the bait truck. There are all kinds of tricks for tough bears, and we create artificial bait hits complete with bear scent from a piece of bear hide. We also burn bacon or honey on bait sites for added effect.

Horace Lane: Our hunters are on the stand about 3:00 P.M., and on the longest day of the year here in Newfoundland, you can stay on the stand until 9:30 with adequate light. Combine that with being up early to help do some baiting, getting back for lunch, and getting prepared for the evening's hunt, and it makes for a long day.

Don Lind: Our usual hunting method is stand hunting, but we often encounter bears feeding along pipeline rights of way or field edges and take those opportunities for spot-and-stalk-style hunting. Occasionally we will also do some spot-and-stalk hunting as a variation to stand hunting, just to change the pace for a hunter.

Claude Turcotte: When I pick a place for a hunter at our initial lunch, I tell the hunter everything I know about how many bears are using the bait, where they'll come from, how many are there, when they'll come in, and so on. We always have a virgin bait for every hunter. Because of this we often have more than 50 percent of our hunters done on the first night. In those huge reserves we hunt, I bait for about two months, and only two nights a year is there a hunter on the stand.

Which season (spring or fall) offers the best hunting in your area? Early or late in the season?

Joe Jakab: Spring generally has a higher success rate, although fall is fun, with hardly any bugs. We can sometimes even do some great spot-and-stalk hunting on blueberry fields in the fall. I also like the end of spring season, when the bear rut has started, which occurs around June 12. Quebec season starts May 15 and ends June 30. I won't take a hunter until about May 27, although baits start getting hit about May 7 and really fire up about May 18.

Horace Lane: I'd recommend the spring, and anytime from the last Saturday in May to the first full week of July. I like that later time slot because you can combine it with a little fishing, but, more importantly, it's the time the bigger bears are more actively mating. They're more likely to make a big mistake then, like the male of any species when he's after females.

Don Lind: Spring season is the best if the hunters want to see a large number of bears. Obviously, by seeing more animals there is a better chance that the hunter will get the trophy he's seeking. The bears are much more active during the spring season for two reasons. First, food sources are scarce, and bears looking for feed will locate our bait sites. By supplying the sites with plenty of feed, we are able to support a number of bears. Secondly, the breeding season for bears is late spring, so that mature, breeding boars travel, trying to locate sows in heat. The boars will hang around our sites for the feed and the potential of finding a "hot" sow. Some hunters prefer fall bears because of the size difference and hair condition. And a bear in the fall can weigh 30 percent more than its springtime weight.

Of course, the head size of the bear does not change from spring to fall, and the weight change is only the result of the increased fat content, stored in the fall for the winter hibernation. Spring hides are very dense, with thick underfur and short guard hairs. A fall hide will not have underfur as dense, but it has more luster and shine than a spring pelt. In the fall you do not get the number of bears at the bait sites because individual bears have located a natural food source over the summer and early fall and they don't stray far as winter approaches. The trophy and overall success rates on our spring hunts are the same in the early or late part of the season.

One of the advantages of an early spring hunt is that if we can locate a specific bear of interest, chances are good that it will remain in the area of the bait site, since food sources are limited and there is no interest in breeding yet. The advantage to a late spring hunt is that you never know where or when the big one might show up. Much like trophy whitetail hunting, mature

A bow hunter is ready! (Photo courtesy of Claude Turcotte)

boars travel great distances looking for female companionship and may hit several sites in an afternoon.

Claude Turcotte: Spring is better because the bears are hungry, and they're on the move during the rut. In the fall they travel less, and it's very hard to keep them on a bait because of all the mature natural foods available. All of our hunts are in the spring, and actually in June, here in Quebec.

Are badly rubbed hides a problem in your area? When is the best time to hunt in order to avoid this problem?

Joe Jakab: I see rubbed hides in young bears and sows starting around June 15, but I have never seen a large male rubbed during the hunting season. All bears seem to have excellent hides in early spring, but all the large males we have taken are prime right through the end of the season. The best hides are spring hides because bears continue to grow hair in their dens through hibernation.

Horace Lane: We have had no more than 5 percent of our hides that present any problem at all, even up into July. In my opinion, the best hides are in the fall, when the hair isn't as long but it's always thick and full. The entire hide is usually pretty lush in the fall, even under the legs and on the belly, places that can be a little thin at times.

Don Lind: Rubbed hides are not a problem in our area, but the hunter has to watch for hide condition prior to shooting. Some bears do come out of the den with rub marks, but that isn't common. As the spring advances and temperatures rise, more rubbed hides show up, but it is usually the younger, immature bears that lose pelt condition first. We have never taken a mature bear, even in late season, with a badly rubbed hide. My sons and I do all of our bear hunting after our spring clients are gone, and we have no problem harvesting mature bears with good pelts.

Claude Turcotte: That is the same everywhere. The hides are better in the spring, but the rubbing also starts in June. The smaller bears rub first, so the big ones will likely have a perfect hide up to the last day of the season. You need to look the bear over before shooting, though, because the hide is the trophy. You want to be sure of it.

What kind of weather is ideal for hunting black bears over bait?

Joe Jakab: I've read that it takes four days of weather at 54 degrees F. to get the bears stirring out of their dens. While hunting I have noticed things going slow when the temperature drops below 54 degrees. Early in the season, cold rain will really slow things down, but later warm rains have no bad effects. Warm and still weather, with a slight drizzle and a dark cloud cover, can really coax a tough bear to wander into your site. Under those conditions, I believe the bears think it's night!

Horace Lane: We find that wind and rain are probably the worst. A warm, muggy day when there's very little wind and the mosquitoes and black flies are swarming unhindered is the best day to hunt bears. I'd prefer a day that's a little dull to a day that's bright and sunny, too.

Don Lind: The best weather for bear hunts is cooler, cloudy conditions, with temperatures in the low to mid-60s. If sky conditions are clear and temperatures are in the 70s, the bears tend to move later in the evening, after temperatures start to drop and the skies darken. Also moister, cooler air seems better for scent attraction. Steady rain will keep most bears in heavy cover for a day or two, but eventually hunger wins out; if the rains continue, they will return to the bait sites.

Claude Turcotte: A temperature range of 75 to 85 degrees seems to be best. If it gets too hot, the bear may come in at night. Wind is the worst problem because they won't come in with a strong wind. Rain doesn't keep them away at all. Warm, but not too warm, and calm, are best.

Give us your perspective on black bear hunting as a game management tool.

Joe Jakab: If bears aren't hunted, they tend to self-regulate the population by dominant boars cannibalizing cubs and young bears. In an unhunted population new bears are born each year, and female cubs are accepted into the range of their mothers as they mature, but male cubs are not. Females have much smaller home ranges, some ten to twenty square miles, whereas dominant males have ranges of from fifty to one hundred square miles. A young male is literally a bear on the run as he tries to find his own home range, and as a result they have a very high mortality. They may end up in direct conflict with the dominant male bear in his range, or else they wind up in the least desirable habitat, in marginal areas that often put them into conflict with people. Hunting is very good for the bear population; a lot of predatory adult males are eliminated directly, and the female to male ratio increases, creating a kind of bear factory with less food competition and more productivity in females. Bears in Ontario mature at about six years of age, while in Pennsylvania it's closer to two and a half to three years. Because of the positive effects of hunting, a hunted population has been known to sustain a harvest of up to 22 percent of the population without reducing the number of bears.

Horace Lane: Hunting is one of the best tools for game management. Here in Newfoundland, the bear is like the lion in Africa: It's the king of the forest, and adults have no predators except for man. Bears are a predator, and they have a bountiful food supply. They eat a lot of berries, which are plentiful here, but also a lot of caribou calves, moose calves, and the like. They do have a tendency to increase in numbers if they aren't hunted, and there's very little hunting pressure from local residents. Having nonresidents come in and hunt is a big plus for bear management, and it's a good management tool.

Don Lind: I strongly believe that baiting for black bears is a significant, necessary, and successful management tool. We have such an abundance of bears in our area that if numbers are not controlled by hunting the resource will necessarily be subjected to serious waste and abuse. Since bears are largely nocturnal mammals that prefer to stay in the confines of heavy cover, they are more difficult to hunt without baiting. Baiting permits hunters to have a high rate of success, and thus populations can be managed effectively. Baiting bears also ensures that sows with cubs are not mistakenly harvested, as the hunter can watch bears up close, and the hunter is not hurried into taking a shot. This up-close inspection also gives the hunter a better look at trophy potential, hair color and condition, and so forth. Many bears may visit a bait site on a given evening, so the hunter has the opportunity to be more selective. If we could not harvest bears by hunting, the population would expand to the extent that bears would become overpopulated for the habitat and start to infringe on the productivity of local beekeepers, crop growers, and cattle ranchers. When that happens, those producers invariably take care of the problem themselves by disposing of the bears, and most of the carcasses go to waste, pelt included.

Claude Turcotte: In my area, we harvest only one bear per twenty-five square kilometers. If you have a good bear population and you manage it conservatively, you won't hurt the population, and you'll always be able to harvest big bears. If you start taking more than that from the area, the average size of the bears you're taking will definitely drop off; you're killing your future when you do that.

Section II

HUNTING WITH HOUNDS

Chapter 7

SELECTING AN OUTFITTER/GUIDE FOR HUNTING WITH HOUNDS

What should a hunter look for when seeking a black bear outfitter/guide?

Wayne Bosowicz: Look for quality references from successful hunters, and equally important, from unsuccessful hunters. Anybody who gets a bear with you will give you a positive reference, of course, but if somebody doesn't get a bear and will still give you a good reference, that really says something. It also helps to have some quality references that are known on a national level. I'd also ask if the guide is full-time or part-time. You can't give a full-time commitment to something you're doing only part-time. Years of experience in this business are also important.

Wade Lemon: If you're hunting with dogs, you really need somebody who's passionate about it. There are a lot of guys with dogs, but very darn few good dog men, who are both dog and bear savvy, and have a passion for hunting bears by this particular method.

Jerry "Finn" Nykanen: The guide's probably going to tell you that he's got everything, and it isn't going to happen. I'd get some references and see how the guy did the year before. Some guides will tell you anything, but if you can check several people who have hunted with a particular guide, you should be able to get some idea of the quality of his operation. We've got a guy up here who's hunted with us most of his life, and now he's a guide for black bears. He takes clients for $2,500 a bear. He got six bears this year, but I'm not aware that he has taken any big ones. So many paying hunters come from the big city; they've never even seen a bear, so they shoot the first one they see. The outfitter should be able to give you some guidance as to the size of the bear in the tree, and with hounds it's pretty easy to look them over. If the bear isn't big enough, take a picture and leave it.

Guide Wayne Bosowicz with some prize hounds. (Photo courtesy of Wayne Bosowicz)

A nice bear taken in Utah with hounds. (Photo courtesy of Wade Lemon)

Mike Richie: I'd look for someone who's been in the business for a while, though there are some new guys who are doing a good job, too. There are too many outfitters out there who are serving the almighty dollar, and it's especially true of bear outfitters, who too often are trying to run as many hunters through their camps as they can. They don't care about quality or mature animals; they just want to take a lot of animals so they can call it a high success rate.

Ideally, a guide should have been in the business for a long time and be willing to give you a lot of references. Be sure to check those references, too, because you can learn a lot from them. Also, select an outfitter who's actually going to be in the field guiding. There are plenty of outfitters who simply book the hunts and then stay at home and collect the money. They hire kids to send out with the hunters, and don't even supervise them to see that they're getting the job done.

What are (a) the most important single characteristic and (b) the worst possible deficiency in a black bear guide?

Wayne Bosowicz: Commitment to getting the hunter a bear would answer the first part; not caring whether the hunter gets a bear would be the second.

Wade Lemon: Knowledge is the single most important qualification for a bear guide, and the lack thereof is the worst deficiency. I'm talking about knowledge of both dogs and the bear. It's extremely important that a guide know what he's doing, and know the habits and ways of the bear. A guy can have a pack of dogs, but if he doesn't understand them he's not going to do a good job for you. We see that a lot. A lot of hound hunters don't understand their dogs well enough to know each particular dog's characteristics—its strengths and weaknesses, and the like.

Jerry "Finn" Nykanen: The main characteristic of a good bear guide is that he likes to hunt bears. If he doesn't like to hunt, and he's in it only for the money, that's the worst deficiency I can imagine. Some guides are charging too much for what they give a client, and that's a bad deficiency, too.

Mike Richie: For hound hunters, the most important characteristic would be persistence and patience, and having really good bear dogs. Keep in mind, though, that the dogs are only as good as the man behind them. If a guy quits his dogs, the dogs are going to start quitting him before long. So he needs to have a lot of heart, a mindset to keep on trying, and a lot of dedication to getting his hunter a bear. I think that the worst possible deficiency is not being personally involved in the hunt, but delegating that responsibility to others, who may or may not be good guides.

Is there any exceptional qualification for being a black bear guide that may not apply to other types of guiding?

Wayne Bosowicz: It all comes down to bear knowledge, whether you're baiting or hound hunting or whatever.

Wade Lemon: The top bear hunters I know are hard-headed enough that they just won't quit. When a bear keeps going and going, a lot of times if you keep on it long enough you'll finally get it in a tree or get it to stop. It's such a tough game that often it's easy to talk yourself into quitting before the bear does.

Wade Lemon says he isn't sure who has who! (Photo courtesy of Wade Lemon)

Jerry "Finn" Nykanen: Not really. Bear hunters are just hunters, and they like to hunt like all hunters.

Mike Richie: Not really, I guess. The only thing that stands out is learning how to judge bears because it's so different from

Some of Jerry "Finn" Nykanen's bear dog houses in Wisconsin. (Photo courtesy of Jerry Nykanen)

judging other animals. Other than that, if a guy is a good guide for other animals, he can be a good black bear guide, too.

What does a good black bear guide do to ensure safety while hunting a uniquely dangerous animal?

Wayne Bosowicz: Keep the client's gun unloaded as long as possible!

Wade Lemon: What worries me more than the bear is the loaded gun. We're using dogs to tell us where the bear is, and it's very important to keep that gun unloaded—or at least, not put a shell in the chamber—until you see the dogs and the bear and you're ready to shoot. Another thing we really try to be aware of is where we are when we shoot the bear. At that point, the bear's mad, he's fighting the dogs, and he's charging. When you shoot him, he really gets mad! It's important to know where he is so that you can keep him from winding you which will allow you to get off a good shot without ever letting him know where you are.

Hometown of Wisconsin bear hunting with hounds. (Photo courtesy of Jerry Nykanen)

Jerry "Finn" Nykanen: I make sure that the guy can shoot, and that he won't shoot me. Be certain that the hunter knows how to load the gun, where the safety is, and how to use it. You really don't want your hunter screwing up once you get to the tree where the bear is. We had one guy shoot a bear in the paw while it was hanging on the tree, and that could have been dangerous. The hunter needs to make a good shot.

Mike Richie: Most of the time when we're hound hunting, it's pretty safe. The only time it can be dangerous is when you get one bayed up on the ground, and you have to sneak your hunter up and try to get a good shot without hitting one of the dogs. If someone wounds a bear, we've got a big advantage with the dogs because we can cut them loose right away and bay the bear again, without someone having to go alone into the brush after him. The dangerous situations develop when the hunter doesn't make a good shot.

Chapter 8
HOUND GUIDES EVALUATE THE HUNTER

What is your favorite type of hunter (personality, physical abilities, experience level, socioeconomic status)?

Wayne Bosowicz: It's our responsibility as guides to make the guest hunter as comfortable and happy as possible. Of course, when it comes to hunters, you have to hunt with what you get. It's not meant as disrespect to anyone, but the average computer expert isn't going to be in the physical condition of a seasoned hound guide. I remember when I first started guiding commercially. I thought I was a big, bad bear hunter, and I'd be first to the tree and shoot the bear. That's a houndsman's mentality speaking. When you're a guide, you learn quickly that you're not in the bear business, you're in the people business—you only think you're in the bear business.

There aren't many people in the world who've been in this business longer than I, and it's because I've learned that it's a people business, not a bear business. You cater to the needs of the hunter. You can want what you want, but as hunters come through the door, you take them the way they are and consider their safety, comfort, and enjoyment. If you get them to the tree where the bear's treed and they have a heart attack, what good is that? You'd like an Olympic contender every time, but that isn't going to happen. The main thing that every guide should remember is this: Without the guest hunter, there would be no work for guides!

Wade Lemon: I like guys from the Southern states, I like Upstate New Yorkers, and I like people from Wisconsin, to name a few. The important thing is attitude. If a guy shows up with a good attitude, he's there for the experience; he enjoys the hunt, enjoys the country, and so on. He asks questions about what

A Wisconsin bear hunt attracts all kinds of hunters. (Photo courtesy of Jerry Nykanen)

we're doing, the plants we encounter, and takes things as they happen. If he's got a good attitude, he doesn't have to go on a set schedule, and he's going to have a good hunt.

Jerry "Finn" Nykanen: I like just an ordinary man, preferably one who hasn't lived in town all of his life and who knows what a bear looks like. I prefer to have a guy who has at least done some deer or bird hunting so that he knows what hunting's all about. If he has even that kind of experience, he knows about gun safety, when to load and when to stay unloaded, and how to keep the thing pointed in the right direction. Above all, I like someone who is safe to hunt with.

Mike Richie: I like a hunter who's enthusiastic about the hunt and in good physical shape. In order for him to enjoy the hunt, and for everybody around him to enjoy it, he's got to be happy to be there. It seems that, more and more today, I see guys showing up who are interested just in the kill—not in the experience and the challenge. I like someone who enjoys being there, enjoys seeing the awesome Selway-Bitterroot Wilderness, and loves hearing the dogs run. Everybody wants to have a successful hunt, but the kind of hunter I like is going to have a successful hunt whether he shoots a bear or not. I like a hunter who understands that being there is a privilege and a pleasure. The kill is just a bonus.

Should inexperienced and physically challenged hunters go hunting for black bears with hounds? Why or why not?

Wayne Bosowicz: That brings up a tough situation, especially the physically challenged part. Inexperience is no problem because almost no client hunter who goes black bear hunting with hounds has ever done it before. The better physical condition a person is in, though, the better experience he can have. For the physically handicapped, I've got some areas that have good road systems, and we can often drive pretty close to where the bear trees. You fit your area to the person you're guiding.

Wade Lemon: I think they should. Of course, with physically challenged hunters, we're very careful where we take them. We'd want an area with good access, so we can get around well with them. As far as inexperienced hunters are concerned, the way you learn is by doing, so there's no problem there.

Jerry "Finn" Nykanen: I'm doing handicapped hunts for deer right now. Wisconsin has a special deal for deer hunting by handicapped hunters, but so far that program isn't for bear hunting. I did take an elderly fellow bear hunting last year, and he couldn't even get to where the bear was treed. But he was able to make a 250-yard shot and kill that bear!

Mike Richie: Inexperienced hunters actually do better with hounds than any other way, in my opinion. If they're sitting over a bait, there's usually nobody there to give them guidance. The hound guide, on the other hand, is always with the client. If the bear is bayed on the ground, it sure makes a difference if you have a hunter with some experience, though. If the bear does the usual and climbs a tree, even the inexperienced hunter can be given plenty of time to look at the bear, get calmed down, and take time in making the shot. Physically challenged hunters can be a problem, but we use horses quite a lot, and it can help if a person can ride. However, even then there's still a certain amount of footwork to be done. Sometimes we get lucky and tree a bear right off the bat, close to the trail, but you can't depend on it. I had a seventy-five-year-old hunter last year on one of the toughest hunts we had, and he made it all the way to the tree, three ridges from where we started. That's another thing I've noticed, that older guys still know how to work. They're from the old school, and they may not be fast, but they'll never quit on you, either; they just keep plugging along. You get a lot of young people today that don't know how to work; when it gets a little tough they turn tail and go home. The older guys generally won't do that.

Is there any particular characteristic in hunters that would make you refuse to guide them on a black bear hunt?

Wayne Bosowicz: We don't take heavy drinkers if we know about it. For handicapped hunters, they still have to be able to walk to a certain extent. Safety, of course, is a priority, but you often don't know how they handle a weapon until you get them in camp, so you deal with it the best you can.

Wade Lemon: If I can spot them, I won't take whiners with a poor attitude! You see it a lot these days. Too many guys want a guaranteed hunt. There may be a time and a place for that kind of thing, and maybe you could guarantee a kill if a person wanted just any bear. But we're hunting big bears, and there are so many variables—weather, scenting conditions—and you're dealing with animals. You've got the bear itself, and you've also got the dogs as variables. Dogs are dogs, and they can reveal faults you didn't know were there at unexpected times. You hear people say that a hunt was poor because they didn't get anything. I don't need that kind of attitude around me anymore.

Jerry "Finn" Nykanen: If the guy is a smart aleck, and he thinks he knows everything even though he's never even been bear hunting, I refuse to take him.

Mike Richie: It's hard to know a lot about a person until you've been around him some, so you're talking about repeat

The best place to start hunting—where there's a bear! (Photo courtesy of Jerry Nykanen)

hunters. I've had some guys in camp that I didn't particularly want to have come back. Usually that's because a person thinks he knows more than the guide and won't listen, and it sure makes for a tough hunt.

What is the most dangerous thing a client can do while hunting black bears with hounds? Can you share an instance in which a client placed himself (or the guide) in danger?

Wayne Bosowicz: The moment you get to the tree is a critical time. Most often the hunter has never seen anything like it before. It's just chaos: The dogs are tied back and screaming, and lots of hunters just can't believe it. Sometimes they start shooting wildly, and even backing up as they shoot. I've even had hunters fall right over backward. More things go on at that tree than anywhere else on a hound hunt. The guide really has to be on his toes because the excitement of the tree can cause

Successful hunters have sometimes followed the hounds for hours. (Photo courtesy of Jerry Nykanen)

the hunter to place everyone there in danger. Also, you've got to look after the safety of the dogs. It's an extremely tense time, and sometimes the hunter comes unglued. The guide has to hold things together.

Wade Lemon: It all boils down to hunters listening to the guide, especially regarding when to shoot and when not to shoot. For example, once the bear is up a tree, I like to tie the dogs back if I can. If the bear's really nervous and we can get a good shot on it, I might not tie them back, but I like to whenever I get the chance. The reason is that if a four-hundred-pound bear falls out of a tree and lands on a dog, that dog is going to be badly hurt or killed.

We had an animal up a mahogany bush once, and I was trying to get the dogs tied back. I'd told the hunter not to shoot until I gave the word, and another guide and I had just reached in to pull two more dogs back when the hunter unexpectedly fired. That critter wound up falling right on the guide's back! He was able to get out from under, but the bear got a dog and bit it pretty badly. It's the old point of waiting until things are right, and having the patience to do so. He might have gotten one of us killed by doing something stupid like that.

Jerry "Finn" Nykanen: Most of the time, when a bear is up a tree it stays there, but a few bears will go up only ten feet or so. When they do that, they're planning to do something that you won't like, such as kill a dog, or get you when you walk up. You've got to be really careful when you go in to the tree if the bear is low like that. You'd like to pull your dogs back, but the bear is so low to the ground that you don't know if he's going to jump on you or jump on a dog. The most dangerous thing a client can do is to beat you to the tree and walk up under a bear that's staying low. He might have that bear jump right on top of him. We've had them jump out and take off lots of times.

Mike Richie: Gun safety is paramount, and today we get far too many hunters who are careless in handling their guns.

A good hunter wants to utilize his kill—in Wisconsin, it's a bear-be-cue! (Photo courtesy of Jerry Nykanen)

These redbone hounds may be contemplating what kind of hunter will be following them. (Photo courtesy of Jerry Nykanen)

Pointing a gun at somebody is the most dangerous thing a hunter can do. We get some hunters who even want to carry a shell in the chamber; we strictly don't allow that. When a guy doesn't listen to the guide, that puts everybody in jeopardy. As far as the bear, we've had very few instances in which there was any real danger. We did have a father and daughter come out a few years ago, and the father had had his daughter practice rapid fire with a .44 Magnum pistol before they left home. We instructed her to take her time and place one round well, but she just blazed away and fired at the bear about eighteen times. She did end up getting the bear, but I kept trying to get her to settle down and make a good shot, while her father was telling her to shoot, shoot, shoot! She had to squeeze off several shots every time. It might have resulted in a wounded bear, but fortunately it turned out all right.

Chapter 9

HOUND GUIDES EVALUATE HUNTING ARMS

What is your favorite rifle caliber for hunting black bears, and do you recommend this caliber for clients?

Wayne Bosowicz: I like the .30-06 or the .45-70. Both are highly popular and eminently adequate for black bears.

Wade Lemon: I like a .25-06 or a 7mm-08. Basically, though, if a bear is in a tree, you can shoot it with absolutely anything and it'll do the job. You want something fairly easy to carry, something that's quick, and that you're comfortable shooting.

The problem is that a lot of these big bear simply won't tree, and you end up baying them and shooting them on the ground. The dogs are in there working the animal up close, and you have dogs all around the bear, both in front of it and behind it. For that reason I prefer a caliber that's not going to go completely through a bear because you can kill a dog on the other side.

Jerry "Finn" Nykanen: My personal favorite is the .30-06, but we let people use whatever they want. Last Saturday we had a guy kill one with a bow, and he made a heck of a shot. It's up to the individual what they shoot, but for me it's a .30-06 with 150-grain bullets.

Mike Richie: There are so many good ones out there. Many of our hunters just use pistols because we aren't shooting long range. I'd say anything between a .30-.30 and a .454 is OK. The .454 now comes in a little lever-action rifle that's really easy to carry, and it sure knocks the heck out of a bear. I carry this caliber in a pistol and it works well. The .30-06 is also really good.

Bowhunting with hounds in Utah is tough because bears often bay on the ground. (Photo courtesy of Wade Lemon)

What is your choice as a backup weapon when guiding for black bears?

Wayne Bosowicz: I use only a handgun, either a .41 or a .44 Magnum.

Wade Lemon: Here in Utah, we're not allowed to carry a gun with a pursuit permit. If we've drawn our own bear tag, we can carry one, though. On the Indian reservations you can carry one, and I usually have with me a .41 Magnum pistol.

Jerry "Finn" Nykanen: Again, the .30-06 is really good. I'd prefer something in the .30-caliber range.

Mike Richie: I carry a .454 pistol most of the time. I also have a .45 lever-action rifle I carry sometimes.

What is your advice on bullet weight? Bullet construction?

Wayne Bosowicz: I strongly prefer heavy-grain bullets, and I don't like hollow points at all. I've field tested a lot of bullets for different companies, testing their actual killing ability, and I've found that the semijacketed softnose bullets do the best job.

Wade Lemon: I don't like hollow points or a ballistic tip. They can explode right in the blubber of these big, fat bears, which may not be fatally wounded after four or five shots. I want more of a solid-type bullet or a Partition-type bullet. I'd recommend the heaviest bullet that the gun is designed to shoot.

Jerry "Finn" Nykanen: Medium bullets of any kind will do the job on a treed bear. Bullet construction doesn't matter much, in my experience. It's a close, easy shot most of the time.

Mike Richie: You need at least a 180-grain bullet in a softpoint or Nosler construction. You sure don't need a steel-jacketed bullet. I use either a 300-grain or a 325-grain bullet in my .454 pistol.

Do you have any tips on shooting techniques in field situations?

Wayne Bosowicz: I would have more to say about shooting in a bait-hunting situation, in which the hunter is shooting down and the bullet can drop a lot. You'd think it would be pretty simple shooting up a tree. I like to make sure that they take a rest and put a good shot on the bear.

Wade Lemon: When the bear is in the tree, there's usually no hurry. You can get all the branches out of the way and have a dead rest. When the bear is on the ground, though, it's an entirely different story. Most of the time we try to get downwind, so we can watch. The bear will be fighting the dogs, popping his teeth, and dogs will be swirling all around him. All of a sudden he'll charge out and scatter the dogs. Then he'll stand there and bounce up and down and pop his teeth, and for just a few seconds before the dogs close back in, and you can get a good shot without endangering the dogs. You need to be able to shoot offhand and shoot quickly in that case.

Jerry "Finn" Nykanen: If the bear has been up there a while, and you can tell by the dogs' barking whether he's up the tree, you have to assess quickly whether the bear might come down.

If he's only run a half-hour, he might very well come down, but if he's been chased two or three hours his tongue is hanging out and he's done running. You've got plenty of time to make the shot, if that's the case. We get our dogs tied back and get the hunter set up to make a good shot with a rest on a tree. Usually he kills the bear and it comes down with a thump. With such close shots as these, there's no excuse for not making a good shot.

Mike Richie: It depends on the situation. If the bear is really far up the tree, we make sure that the hunter gets a good rest on something, and make sure that they don't rest the barrel against a tree. A lot of guys bring pistols, usually with open sights, but we have plenty of hunters who bring rifles. The shot is almost anticlimactic in hound hunting, so it isn't the big deal it might be in spot-and-stalk or bait hunting. We've got plenty of time after we finally reach the tree.

What advice do you give your hunters on shot placement on a black bear?

Wayne Bosowicz: Depending on the gun, you can actually put a shot through both shoulders and get the heart, liver, and lungs in one crack. The hunter needs to come in behind a treed bear and angle the bullet up from the shoulders, and it can then even skip up into the head: You can truly get all the vitals with one shot.

Wade Lemon: I may give advice that's different from what hunters are used to getting. When we're hunting these big bears, and they're on the ground fighting the dogs, I just basically want them to get a bullet in the animal. When they're in a tree, I want the shot through the chest, through the shoulder, neck, or throat—whatever the presentation allows. You've got to sort through the branches of the tree and find the vital zone. Naturally a clean kill is always preferable, but if that bear is on the ground, just shoot him wherever you can and start to break him down. You train all your life not to take a shot unless it's a good one, but the difference here is the dogs. In this situation it's critical to shorten up the process by whatever means you can.

A bear in a tree can be an easy shot—or an impossible one! (Photo courtesy of Jerry Nykanen)

Jerry "Finn" Nykanen: I'm a lung shooter, but usually when a bear's up a tree, you can angle it upward through the lungs and get the opposite shoulder as well.

Mike Richie: If the bear is in a tree, as they usually are, I have the hunter place the shot just behind the shoulder into the heart-lung area. If the animal is bayed up on the ground and we can get a broadside shot, I try to put it right through the shoulders, to break them down and protect the dogs a little. A heart-lung shot at a bear on the ground isn't dangerous to the hunter particularly, but it can sure get some of the dogs torn up. That bear is fighting mad, even though it's dying.

How many of your first-time black bear hunters are intimidated by the prospect of hunting a dangerous animal? Describe some typical such reactions.

Wayne Bosowicz: Not many hunters come into camp with any degree of apprehension, but they sure can get that way when

Any legal weapon can take a nice bear when it's treed—good shot placement saves dogs. (Photo courtesy of Jerry Nykanen)

they actually see the bear. Things can get wild when you take a hunter, for the first time in his life, up to a tree with a bear in it.

Wade Lemon: You get some apprehension, but most guys are pretty well prepared psychologically. What most hunters worry about is whether the bear is going to charge through the dogs, or whether it might come down the tree at them. In one case we had a hunter who had already killed his bear, and we were just training dogs. We had a big old black bear on a private ranch, one we called "Gentle Ben." We don't get many black bears because most are chocolate or cinnamon in color. This was a unique situation because we knew the bear; it was big and mellow and always easy to catch.

Well, we caught the bear, and I sent the hunter down the canyon after the dogs while I was going to drive down to the other end and come up that way with the truck. I had just gotten started when the hunter came on the radio and called, "Wade, get down here!" He wouldn't say why, so I stopped the truck and plunged off the steep canyon wall. When I got down there I could see the bear in a tree, with the dogs all around, and this guy's video camera lying on the ground. He stuck his head out of some brush and reached for his camera, and the bear slapped the tree trunk with his paw, sending bark flying, and then gave one of those big "Woof, woof, woof!" sounds. That guy turned inside out diving back into the brush, and dropped his camera again! It was hilarious!

Jerry "Finn" Nykanen: The reactions are sometimes unbelievable, but I don't think they are really intimidation. We had a seventeen-year-old girl, a senior in high school, who came with us and killed her first bear. She was the happiest little thing I've ever seen. If a person doesn't get a little excited, they don't deserve to be hunting! I've never had anyone get so excited or scared that they shot up in the air or anything. Nobody we've guided has been totally inexperienced with hunting, so we get very little real fear. We had one guy that shot the bear in the paw, but fortunately we got the bear good when it came down.

Mike Richie: You get some guys who come out thinking that black bears are really dangerous—and they can be in some situations. Our advantage is that when we're hound hunting, we're always with the hunter, so we can provide guidance and help to avoid trouble. In bait hunting, a cub can come in, and some people will think that it's a big old grizzly bear. We don't have to deal with that, though we do on occasion put an out-of-shape or disabled hunter over bait. We've even had a few guys insist that we sit right there with them when they're hunting over bait!

How do you prepare for and handle overpowering excitement in a hunter/client?

Wayne Bosowicz: That's a tough one. I just make them keep their gun unloaded until they calm down. Most people with that problem are in awe at the methods we use hunting with hounds because it's so different from what they'd expected. I use a strike dog riding on the top of the truck. I'll describe it for you later.

Wade Lemon: I think that the best thing is to carry the gun for a hunter like that, because too much excitement can be a dangerous thing. If there's no bullet in the chamber until it's time to shoot, you have eliminated a lot of potential problems, and at that time, you just tell the hunter to shoot the bear. It's a lot like calling coyotes, where if you watch that animal coming in for miles and miles, you can let the excitement get to you and completely miss the shot. If, on the other hand, it presents suddenly without your being aware that it's there, you usually make a good shot because you don't have time to get excited. We try to do that with our hunters if they seem excitable; by the time they see the bear, it's time to shoot.

Jerry "Finn" Nykanen: You want to see some excitement, as I said, but sometimes you have to tell people to settle down. It usually isn't a problem. People sure need to respect a bear in a tree, though, because they can come down in a second or two, with bark flying in all directions.

Mike Richie: I just sit them down for a minute and tell them to relax and think about what they're doing. Usually we have time to make sure that they've settled down. When the dogs tree, some hunters want to run right in there and see what's happening. We have to hold them back to make sure the bear is really treed, and not just temporarily bayed up, and that the bear doesn't bail out of the tree and take off again. We use a lot of talking to get the hunter relaxed and settled before it comes time for a shot.

Do you have any wise words on bowhunting? Black-powder hunting?

Wayne Bosowicz: Seeing as I'm still in business, I do, of course. Archers need heavy, wide broadheads, and I've seen them do the job with just one shot. Both black-powder hunters and bow hunters do well on our hunts. It really boils down to the same old story of shot placement on the very first try. Both types of hunters have trouble getting off a second shot.

Even crossbows can take a treed bear if the situation is right. (Photo courtesy of Mike Richie)

With a modern rifle hunter, it's easy to put a second shot in immediately, but with the bow or the black-powder gun, it isn't that quick. Everybody's first shot is the most important, but it's critical for the bow hunter and the black-powder hunter to make a good first shot.

Wade Lemon: My wise word for the bow hunter is "Get a gun." I'm kidding, and we take a lot of archery hunters, but if something's going to go wrong, it can do so much more easily if the hunter is using a bow. We tell everybody that if they bring a gun and they get in a bind, we'll help them carry it. But if they bring a bow, they're on their own! We've had quite a few black-powder hunters, and they generally do very well. Both types of hunters need to be practiced and ready because Utah state law doesn't allow us to carry a backup weapon for them.

Jerry "Finn" Nykanen: We have had a few bow hunters, and they've all done really well. We haven't had any black-powder hunters.

Mike Richie: We do take both kinds of hunters. Bow hunters who hunt with hounds should practice shooting acutely uphill, or maybe actually put a target up in a tree. Sometimes those bears will get up quite a ways, and the hunter will overshoot or undershoot because he's not used to shooting up at such a steep angle. It can be tricky. Most of the time you can get up the hill and shoot more or less level at the bear, but sometimes that's not possible; they need to be ready. Black-powder hunters should have some way to keep their powder dry because we do get rain in the Selway. I had a guy a couple of years ago who just couldn't get his black-powder weapon to fire, and he used up all but his last primer. He unloaded the gun, manually dried it out, reloaded, and finally was able to shoot the bear using his last cap. By that time I was really beginning to wonder.

Do you take any special precautions when hunting with bow hunters or black-powder hunters?

Wayne Bosowicz: No matter what hunter I'm guiding, I've got my handgun ready right at the bottom of the tree. If that bear comes down wounded, he's going to get "whifted." I'm always prepared for that very situation.

Wade Lemon: Bow hunters are more of a problem than black-powder hunters. For example, if you've got a bear lying in a tree, I especially want to get those dogs tied back before the bow hunter shoots. The reason is that I've lost two dogs as a result of bowhunting bears. The arrow doesn't pass clear through, and the bear hits the ground and runs. We then turn loose a couple of dogs to chase it down. I've had several dogs run up to the bear and impale themselves on the arrow sticking out of the bear, even after it's already dead, and, as I said, two died. I like to have the arrow pass through completely and then actually find the arrow before turning my dogs loose.

Jerry "Finn" Nykanen: We back up the bow hunters pretty well. A very recent hunter killed a bear with a bow and made a great shot at the animal, which was about fifty feet up the tree. The arrow went all the way through the bear and was sticking out the other side. When the bear hit the ground, the arrow popped right out. But we're ready with our weapons if a dangerous situation should develop.

Mike Richie: We don't usually take special precautions unless there's a bay-up on the ground, where I'd sure prefer not to have a bow hunter. The problem is that when they're bayed on the ground, you can't get the dogs back, and a bow hunter isn't going to be able to break the bear down and give the dogs a better chance of surviving. Other than in a situation like that, I don't do anything different.

Chapter 10

HUNTING BLACK BEARS WITH HOUNDS

What is the most common mistake made by guided black bear hunters using hounds?

Wayne Bosowicz: Thinking that it's easy. Hunting black bears with hounds is probably the toughest hunt there is.

Wade Lemon: It's the guide, not the hunter, who makes most of the mistakes in this game. You're dealing with trained animals when you hunt with dogs, and things don't always go just right. You can sometimes bay up a bull elk or a bull moose instead of a bear! That's especially true when you're training a bunch of young dogs as you go along. I've had that happen, and if it's late in the day I've even sent the hunter back to camp, thinking that all the dogs have probably quit. Then while I'm trying to gather them up, I find that they've got a bear bayed! That's been the most common mistake I've made—assuming that the dogs have quit when most of them are out there doing exactly what I want them to do.

Jerry "Finn" Nykanen: Rushing in to the tree is dangerous, although it doesn't happen very often that the hunter is the first one there. If you rush in to the tree the bear will see you, and then it's either going up higher or coming down. It would be a terrible mistake if the hunter got there first and shot the bear before we could tie back the dogs because we'd surely lose a dog or two if he didn't make a good shot.

Mike Richie: It's so much more forgiving when you're with hounds, and your biggest problem is just getting to the tree. The biggest mistake hound hunters make is not being in good enough physical shape to get to the tree. That's especially critical when there's a bay on the ground and you've got to move to get there and get a shot. It's usually the really big bears that just won't

Mike and Dawn Richie with some of their hounds and a big bear. (Photo courtesy of Mike Richie)

climb a tree, so when they bay on the ground, it's critical to get there as fast as you can, or they're off to the races again. We had a big bear bayed up a couple of times, and the hunter had his pistol in his backpack. Every time we got near it, he couldn't get the pistol out in time to shoot. I finally handed him my pistol about the fourth time we bayed the bear, and he killed the animal with it.

What can guided hunters do that would most improve their chances of taking their game (patience, physical fitness, mental preparation, equipment, practice with choice of weapon)?

Wayne Bosowicz: Patience and physical fitness top the list in my book.

Wade Lemon: It sure pays to be in good shape, or at least in the best shape possible. It's also important to know your weapon and what you're capable of doing with it. Also important are walking quietly and checking the wind so you know where your scent is going.

Jerry "Finn" Nykanen: It's good to be able to walk, although most of our bears tree and we can usually get in fairly close. If you're a couple of hundred pounds overweight, though, it's still going to be a tough hunt for you. The other things aren't nearly as important.

Mike Richie: With our type of hunting, you can't beat being in good physical condition. You won't do much sitting when you're hunting bears with hounds.

Besides the weapon, what kind of equipment should every hunter carry? Besides the weapon, what is the most important single piece of equipment?

Wayne Bosowicz: A knife and compass are both essential in this game.

Wade Lemon: A sharp knife, a flashlight, and a camera are all important. The most important single piece of equipment is a sharp knife because you can be pretty sure the guide isn't going to have one!

Jerry "Finn" Nykanen: Always take a camera, and take a picture of the bear in the tree and some more when you get it on the ground. Here in Wisconsin you've got to have a back tag with a number on it, just like when you're deer hunting. It's kind of like a prisoner's number, and is issued by the Department of Natural Resources. It shows that you've bought a license, and it was designed so that someone could easily get your number if you do something wrong. As far as equipment is concerned, a handheld radio really helps in some instances. These days we've got radios in the trucks, radio collars on the dogs, and a lot of other things we didn't used to have.

Mike Richie: A flashlight is a very important item to have along, or even two of them, and some extra batteries. Most of the time we're not coming back in the dark, but when we do, they're essential. Hunters should also carry matches and some fire-starting material, should they somehow become separated or otherwise stranded for the night. Sometimes we do split up when we go to check on the dogs, and it's sure best to have a way to keep yourself comfortable. We carry radios for safety, but even if we're in radio contact a fire can make the difference between comfort and misery. You need good waterproof boots and a good set of rain gear, too, because rain is a fact of life in the Selway.

Are there any common items of equipment that you feel are unnecessary, redundant, or just plain worthless for hunting black bears with hounds?

Wayne Bosowicz: Many hunters bring too much. You should carry only the basics. This is a sweat-and-blood type of hunt, so everything needs to be lightweight. It's even best to have a small camera belt that doesn't weigh much. You move much better if you aren't weighed down with a whole lot of unnecessary stuff.

Wade Lemon: I can't think of anything totally worthless at the moment.

Jerry "Finn" Nykanen: We had one guy who brought a pistol on each thigh, pistols on both sides of his belt, and more darned armament than anybody would ever need. It's a wonder he didn't drop before he got to the tree, with all the stuff he carried. All you need is one weapon you can shoot well, not an armload of them.

Mike Richie: Some guys show up with rangefinders and the like, and those aren't necessary, except maybe for bow hunters. Most people bring far too many clothes. They end up hunting in the same outfit most of the time, but they've got a duffel full of clothes.

Tell us your method of field judging black bears for size.

Wayne Bosowicz: That's a bitter pill, because ground shrinkage is a real problem with all black bears. They look like they weigh 500 pounds while they're in the tree, and they feel like

800 pounds if you carry them out. But when you put them on the scale, they weigh 150 pounds, and that's tough. The thing with hound hunting, as well as with bait hunting, though, is that you really do have the time to look the bear over. The head size, ear size, foot size, and so on can be deceptive. I tell my hunters to look the animal over, and if it's a mature animal they're satisfied with, to shoot it. If not, we'll go looking for another.

Wade Lemon: Utah has some of the biggest black bears in the world. Five or six of the top ten in the book have come out of Utah, and there are only forty to fifty bears killed here annually. We hunt more for tracks than for anything else. I try to find a front paw print, and if you get a track pushing six inches, you know you've really got something.

Also, you can somewhat tell the weight of a bear by the impression the animal makes on the ground, and by the way the feet splay outward with the weight. When you get one of these bears that weigh between four hundred and five hundred pounds, you can really read how heavy the animal is. They just blow the dust right out to the side by the compression of their feet. Under the pines it's tough to see a track, but you can see impressions in the pine needles where a very heavy bear has passed.

At the tree, you look at the size of the head, though it can be somewhat deceiving. You want to look for small ears relative to head size as another indicator. Something I think is more reliable than the ears is the wrists, if I can get around to where I can see them well. The sows will usually have smaller wrists than the boars. If the bear is on the ground, you just compare the size of the bear with the size of the dogs.

Jerry "Finn" Nykanen: I'll start answering this one by telling you that, in my opinion, our Department of Natural Resources has an awful lot of people who don't know what they're doing. The guys running things are kids who've never seen a bear in the wild, and they're all from Oshkosh or Milwaukee or Madison or somewhere. In fact, we've been taking all the new wardens hound hunting, to get a bear up a tree, so they can see one. Then they'll tell you the smaller the ears, the bigger the bear, but that's totally wrong.

A big Selway-Bitterroot Wilderness bear taken after a hard chase over rough country. (Photo courtesy of Mike Richie)

I've got a bear living right behind my cabin that weighs five to six hundred pounds, and his ears are as big as my hand. Ears don't mean anything. You've got to look at body size. If they're sitting in the crotch of a tree kind of hunched over, it can be really hard to judge the size. If they're hanging on the side of the tree like a squirrel, though, you can judge pretty well. Also, a big bear has huge arms, and if it's a really big bear you don't have to look a second time. Skull size means very little because some of the biggest bears have small heads.

Mike Richie: The easiest way is to look at the ears. Generally, if a bear has big ears, it's a small bear; if he's got little ears, he's a big bear. When you get a big bear treed, you get a chance to study it a little bit, and the ears have been the most reliable way for us to tell the big ones from the medium-size or small ones. If you've got one up a tree, that's certainly true. If you see a bear walking across a canyon, it's easier to tell because you can watch the way it moves. A big bear is very deliberate and lumbers along slowly, but a small bear or a sow is light on its feet and makes a lot of jerky movements.

What is the most reliable way to determine sex when no cubs are present? Give us some other methods as well.

Wayne Bosowicz: I don't know of any perfectly reliable method. In the ideal situation, you might be able to see a sow's nipple line or something else to tip you off. Usually the hunter is too excited to make a judgment like that. In most instances, the cubs are close by, either in a nearby tree or in the same tree as the mother, and that cinches it. You gather up your dogs and get out of there.

Wade Lemon: On boars, if they're in a tree, you can see their testicles most of the time. On a sow, if she's got cubs around, you can usually see her nipples. As I said before, sows have smaller wrists than boars, if you can get a look at them. They also have smaller heads.

Jerry "Finn" Nykanen: Cubs are naturally the best way. We've seen as many as five cubs up the tree with the mother bear at one time. The head size is important, too, because sows have much smaller heads. A boar will be longer by as much as two feet. Sows are stockier, though, because they're like a lot of women—they put on six inches or more of lard around the rear. A boar will seldom have more than three inches.

Mike Richie: The head of a sow is more slender than a big boar's head. The sow also has much smaller and tighter feet, while those of a big boar are more spread out. The sheer size will often tell you it's a boar, and sometimes you can see the sex organs while they're up a tree.

How do you normally proceed to follow up after a shot at a black bear?

Wayne Bosowicz: If the guy makes a good shot, we just skin the bear out right there, especially if it's a really big bear.

Excited dogs treed on a nice bear far back in the Selway-Bitterroot Wilderness.
(Photo courtesy of Mike Richie)

We take the hide, and I quarter up the bear so the hunter can take some of the meat home.

Wade Lemon: Of course, if the bear's up a tree, we try to get the dogs tied back, away from the tree. If the bear's up a tree when it's shot and it takes off, I turn loose a couple of young dogs first. They aren't bold enough to charge right in, but they'll let us know where it is.

Jerry "Finn" Nykanen: We make sure it's dead first. We did have one come roaring at the hunter, and the backup man had to shoot it in the neck to kill it. When we're sure it's done, we gut it right away, so it's a little easier to drag out. We make some of the best sausage in the world out of our bears. You have to put a little pork in with it, but it's just delicious. We also have a few bear feeds every year for the local folks.

Mike Richie: When we have a bear treed but before the shot, we always leash up the dogs and tie them back away from the tree for their own protection. If the bear's hit hard by the shot, it usually ends up rolling down the hill a good ways because you wouldn't believe the location of some of the trees these Selway bears climb. I leave the dogs leashed up, and I make sure the bear's dead before I unleash them. If I can't find the bear I assume it's wounded, and we turn the dogs loose to try to bay it up on the ground, or, if it's able, to get it to climb another tree. It's a bad situation when they're wounded enough that they won't climb a tree because that's when they're likely to kill a dog or two.

What procedure do you follow when you know a black bear is wounded?

Wayne Bosowicz: With hounds, it's simple if the bear gets away from the tree. I try not to let that happen, though. I'm right there at the bottom of the tree, and if it comes down wounded or with a lot of life left in it, I'm going to nail it. If one does get by me, the hounds get released again and I hope that the bear has the strength to climb another tree. It's trouble if he can't; then it's out come the sutures for the dogs.

Wade Lemon: We simply let the dogs run them down again. That happens occasionally, even when a bear's shot while in a tree. That's the nice thing about the dogs—that is, the bear isn't going to get away wounded.

Jerry "Finn" Nykanen: If the bear really gets away, which has never happened, we'd just turn the dogs loose after it again.

Mike Richie: If it's wounded and still traveling, I just turn the dogs loose, and they catch up to it pretty quickly. I've had people who have been hunting over a bait come to me after they wound a bear, even a day or two later.

Chapter 11

SPECIFIC GUIDING AREAS FOR HUNTING WITH HOUNDS

Describe your home guiding area for hunting black bears, and any distinctions that set it apart.

Wayne Bosowicz: I guide in Maine and in Ontario, both of which are thickly forested where the bears live. It's the same situation everywhere there are black bears: Food is the key to finding them. In spring, bears eat a lot of grass, and in fact they eat it year-round to some extent, so we go where there's grass in order to hunt them. Later, different types of berries become important—first strawberries, then raspberries, blackberries, cherries, and so on. In fall, beechnuts are a prime food source for bears. I think bears are kind of like me—food dictates to their brains!

Wade Lemon: Around Ferron, Utah, it looks like a smaller version of the Grand Canyon. It's really an unusual place. The type of bear we have here is also unusual because it's bigger, meaner, and, I think, genetically different from anyplace else. I mentioned that only forty to fifty bears are killed by sportsmen in Utah every year, and five to ten of them will make the Boone and Crockett record book. That's a very high percentage. Additionally, the terrain here is different. There aren't many roads, but there are a lot of canyon rims that are incredible. I've seen bears go off into places where you simply can't follow. Just last week we had a bear go into one of those places, and we had to go back the next day with one hundred feet of rope to retrieve four dogs that had slid down to a place they couldn't get out of by themselves. It's really rough country, and the bears have learned how to use it to their advantage. The bears here eat a lot of domestic sheep and some cattle, plus pine nuts, berries of various kinds, acorns, and the like.

On the Indian reservations things are a little different, and the bears eat a lot of juniper berries; they also eat prickly pear and pine nuts.

Jerry "Finn" Nykanen: It's rolling terrain with lots of rivers and lakes. It's pretty thick country, with plenty of trees and brush. It's ideal bear habitat.

Mike Richie: The Selway-Bitterroot Wilderness is the third largest wilderness area in the Lower Forty-eight, consisting of some 1.3 million acres, mostly in Idaho but also spilling over into Montana. It varies from open pine hillsides to really thick, brushy cover. It's a rough place that has tremendously varied habitat. There are areas that are exceptionally dry, and other areas that are virgin rain forest–type of terrain.

What kind of area is ideal for hunting black bears with hounds?

Wayne Bosowicz: A place that's got lots of roads!

Wade Lemon: An area that has a lot of roads is ideal.

Jerry "Finn" Nykanen: The area we hunt is about ideal: mixed woods, rolling hills, and some streams. It also helps to have a lot of old logging roads for access.

Mike Richie: It's all in the eyes of the beholder. The Selway is pretty ideal, in my opinion, because the bears have plenty of food and cover, and there are probably more bears there than anywhere else in the state of Idaho. There is a tremendous variety in the vegetation, and that makes for good feeding by bears. The Selway also has plenty of horse trails, so you can get around in it. It's not an area full of roads where you can run your dogs right off the back of the pickup, but that's part of what makes it special. Our dogs might run five or six miles or more before they even hit a track, and then the chase begins from there. So your dogs have to be in tremendous physical shape, probably more so than anywhere else where there's hound hunting. I think it's ideal, but it is rough; you need to be in good physical condition to really enjoy hunting there. One problem we can have in the spring is the many creeks and rivers we sometimes need to cross. We have to be careful if the water's really high, which it sometimes is.

Describe your pack of black bear hounds—type, training, care. Do you ever lose hounds to bears while hunting? Are there any unusual characteristics or individual antics in the group?

Wayne Bosowicz: We use Plott hounds, a tremendously fast dog that runs with the head up. Just as there are good people and bad people, it's the same with hounds. I've hunted with black-and-tan hounds, blue tick hounds, and others, but I was always particularly pleased with Plotts because of their speed and style of running. I have occasionally lost dogs to bears—a couple of times I never even saw the kill because it would happen during the chase: The bear would just whirl around and nail a dog. Dogs are all different, just like people. When I've got a good group of hounds together, my philosophy is never to break up the group, and never to add a dog to it nor subtract one, if possible. Even if there's a dog that you think isn't making much of a contribution, if the pack is clicking, don't mess with it! It's a very complicated dynamic, and you should never interfere.

Wade Lemon: I'm kind of partial about the type of dogs I hunt. Mine are crossbred to put certain characteristics in them. They have a blue tick base, but you'd never know that by looking at them. They're redder, and some are speckled. I crossed some trig hound into them a few years ago, and that's a running type of dog used to chase coyotes. A lot of my dogs show the trig characteristic of a white ring around their neck. I hunt nearly every day, and I've got to have a dog with really tough feet to do that. The Walker type of hound is pretty good, but their feet just won't hold up. They've got to have a long period of rest between chases or they wind up crippled. I've run a truckload of Plott hounds, and gosh, I don't think a guy could run fast enough to give me another Plott, for two reasons: They don't have a good enough nose to hunt our country, and they're just mean, dog-fighting sons-of-guns. I want a dog that's really cold-nosed, and yet is fast enough to hang with a bear all day and finally

A big Utah bear taken with hounds and bow. (Photo courtesy of Wade Lemon)

catch up. It's a hard combination to get. I don't know why, but lion scent will hold on the ground longer than bear scent. Your dogs will take an old lion track and do something with it, but it's hard to get dogs to follow a cold bear track, for some reason. The ideal pack would have every dog able to do it all, but you don't usually get that. Our dogs have to be well disciplined in this canyon country, and you've got to keep control of them. The old hound hunter Phil Taylor used to put it like this: You can take those dogs hunting, or they can take you hunting!

Jerry "Finn" Nykanen: We've got a variety of dogs, including Walkers, blue tick, black-and-tan, and so on. I don't like Plott hounds because all you get is a big fight at the base of the tree. Above all, you've got to have at least a few dogs that will bite the bear right in the rear. If you don't have some dogs that will do that, the bear will stay on the ground and run all day. Somebody's got to really bite him. When we skin out our bears, sometimes it looks like they've been shot in the butt with buckshot, just from where the dogs have bitten them. There are bloodshot areas all over the rump, and that's the kind of pressure you've got to have to get the bear

Moose Creek Ranger Station in the vast Selway-Bitterroot Wilderness—heart of bear country in Idaho. (Photo courtesy of Mike Richie)

to tree. I've had only one bear dog I'd call a "million dollar dog." Everybody ought to have at least one dog like that in a lifetime. He did it all, and won every competition I ever put him in.

Mike Richie: I run pretty much all blue ticks. They're out of Michigan, from a fellow named Dave Dean. Dave did more for the blue tick breed than anybody in history, and he took them to a whole new level. He built them into the ideal trail and tree dog, with an awful lot of stamina, determination, and will power that really sets the breed apart. My dogs aren't what you'd call gritty bear dogs that are in there biting the bear in the butt all the time, but I don't really want mine to do that. They can get hurt that way. They will bite a bear, but it's not their normal way. When you run too many dogs, or have dogs that are too aggressive, they end up running in and getting hurt. If that happens they can end up being whipped off bears and not want to run them. I've got a few Walker hounds that a good friend raises for me. I keep eight to ten hounds, but most of the time I run only three or four. I think you have more trouble with hurt dogs when you run a bunch, because the more dogs there are the more chance that bear has to grab one and either chew it up or kill it.

Bears are a lot more dangerous to the dogs than cougars are, and I've lost several to bears over the years. I lost a really good female hound to a bear a couple of years ago. I'd gone to help a guy who'd wounded a bear off a bait, and we caught up to that one for him. We jumped another bear off a different bait while we were coming back, and we treed it pretty quickly. I think it was a bear I'd treed a few days earlier. When I got to the tree, it was acting really strangely, standing there in the tree all nervous and popping its teeth. We jumped him, and he ran and bayed, then ran again and bayed, and finally put up a fight. He shut up three of my best dogs, and the female chased him down into the bottom. He killed her right there. I didn't find her for a couple of days. She got swiped really hard, and it killed her.

Describe your typical camp setup and camp routine.

Wayne Bosowicz: We have really nice camps with television, showers, housekeeping, and all the amenities. We're up before daylight, and often we're out until long after dark.

Wade Lemon: We do more camping out of motel rooms and cabins on private ground, depending on the situation. We get up and have breakfast early and get ready to go.

Jerry "Finn" Nykanen: We've got a cabin out back where our hunters stay, and it's pretty nice.

Mike Richie: We set up all tents because we have to fly everything in there—it's a designated wilderness. We've got several different places we camp, and we try to move around to rotate the areas we're hunting. We've got wall tents with internal frames and a wood stove, and wood floors in them, with cots to sleep on. It's about as comfortable as you can make it in a true wilderness area: There's a light on the table, and a drying rack so you can hang up your clothes at night if you get wet. There's also a cook tent and a guide tent.

We leave camp most of the time right around 8:00 A.M., unless it's really hot, in which case we leave even earlier. It takes some time to get the horses ready, and while the hunters are having breakfast we're working on that. Actually it's not bad if it is a little hot because those bears tend to move around better in a little warmth.

What is your success rate on trophy animals?

Wayne Bosowicz: That's a real tough question because to me they're all trophies, whether they're record-book quality or not. Some of the toughest bears are those little one hundred-pound females that can be running and fighting dogs every second; a three-hundred-pounder may go up a tree right away. Most all of our hunters get a chance at a bear.

Wade Lemon: It's about 95 to 98 percent. We try to know where the big ones are, and we hunt them pretty hard.

Jerry "Finn" Nykanen: Everybody who hunts a bear with us kills one.

Mike Richie: Most of the time we're 100 percent. Sometimes it's 90 percent because not everybody will stay with it until they get their bear. It seems like every year we have a week or so when the bears really want to run, and that makes it really tough. Before and after that it's easier. Our season opens April 1 and runs to June 30. I usually don't even start hunting until toward the end of April, when all the bears are out and moving.

Describe your usual hunting method and any common variations.

Wayne Bosowicz: I always have a specific region I'm going to hunt, so I just hitch a dog up on top of the truck and we drive along looking for that strike. The dog will let you know when a bear has crossed. When that happens, I turn that dog loose to straighten out the track, and then add other dogs appropriately. The plan then is to follow the pack to the tree, though often it isn't that simple.

Wade Lemon: Here in Utah, we can't turn the dogs loose before daylight, so I want to be in the area at daylight. We have some strike dogs rigged, but we also look for tracks. Sometimes we drag the roads the day before so we can see any fresh track that crosses. If we haven't found anything like that by 11:00 A.M.,

In some areas pickups can be used for access—in other places, it's horses or walking. (Photo courtesy of Mike Richie)

we walk canyons and let the dogs hunt ahead of us. If they strike a track, it's off to the races.

Jerry "Finn" Nykanen: We've gone to using bait stations to start our hunt. We used to look for tracks, but it's easier to tell what you're chasing if you check a bait station and discover what's been using it. We all fan out and check baits until somebody finds a big track. You can't always judge how big the bear will be by the track size, but it's a good place to start. We then turn the dogs loose, and away we go.

Mike Richie: We put out some baits and sometimes run bears off them. I prefer, though, to strike a track as we move along the horse trail. The baits can be a problem because sometimes there are two or three bears on a bait, and all of a sudden you've got dogs going in three different directions. Generally, though, we put out a couple of strike dogs running free, and we often lead a couple of dogs with the horses. We ride the ridge trails until we hit a fresh track. If a guy wants to sit on a bait in the evening after we get back in, we can do that, too. We often don't know what size bear it is until we get it up a tree, though sometimes we might see

Packing into hound hunting camp in the huge Selway-Bitterroot Wilderness of Idaho. (Photo courtesy of Mike Richie)

a track or see the bear, depending on the terrain we're in. Once your dogs are off and running, you've got to tree the bear in order to retrieve the dogs.

Which season (spring or fall) offers the best hunting in your area? Early or late in the season?

Wayne Bosowicz: Spring is the best time to hunt a bear. Unlike any other animal, black bears do not have their young in the spring, but in the fall after they enter the den. They breed from mid-June into July, and have around a seven-month gestation period. In the spring, therefore, a bear is not pregnant. When you hunt them in the fall, and shoot a sow, she may very well be pregnant. No lawmaker in the world would let that kind of hunt take place for deer or moose, or anything else, but with bears they just seem to ignore biological facts. If your state or province really wants to look after the bear population, they should allow only spring hunting. The facts speak for themselves. Some 80 percent of bears taken in the spring are males, but in the fall it's darn close to 50–50 male to female. A few years ago Quebec eliminated the fall hunt and went with the spring hunt only. Quebec refused to give in to the bleeding heart groups, and went on sound biological data to make that decision. No other state or province has had the guts to do it, but that's the best way to go. Of course, bear hides are the best in the spring.

Wade Lemon: Here in Utah we have both a spring and a fall season, and the two are equally good for big bears.

Jerry "Finn" Nykanen: We only have a fall season, about six weeks long. The later in the season you hunt, the better the hides, of course.

Mike Richie: I like spring the best, though I think that the bears are better able to run hard in the spring because they're leaner. In spring the bears are all more congregated, too, because the first thing they do is to come down to the lower country along the river to get to the fresh green growth. In the fall they're spread all over the place and they're up high, but it's a little easier chasing them because they're carrying more weight and won't run as far. In the spring, anytime after the weather warms up, the bears are more active, but you've got to be ready for a longer chase to catch up to them.

Are badly rubbed hides a problem in your area? When is best to hunt in order to avoid this problem?

Wayne Bosowicz: No. If they were, I couldn't hunt. Spring is the best time to avoid the problem altogether, wherever you hunt—or as late as possible in the fall.

Wade Lemon: The spring season ends on the first of June, so rubbed hides aren't a problem then. Our bears don't start rubbing off their winter coats until the middle of June. The fall season starts the first of August and goes to October. It's best to wait until later in September before hunting because in August and the first of September the hides aren't rubbed but also they're not as thick and full as they are a little later.

Jerry "Finn" Nykanen: The only hides that are a problem are those on bears that have been interfering with someone's bird field, or have been someplace else they shouldn't, and have been shot in the butt with birdshot. They lose all the hair on the rump wherever the shot hits, I guess because it itches. Rubbed hides are otherwise not a problem for us.

Mike Richie: It isn't a big problem. It seems like a lot of the little bears are badly rubbed, but those aren't the bears we kill. That's another advantage of hunting with hounds because you can look them over in the tree and pass up any bear that has bad rubs. With other types of hunting you may not get such a good look until after you've shot the bear. But you're never likely to find any significant rubs on a really big boar bear. A big bear has learned to take better care of itself, while little bears sometimes come out of the den with rubs all over them. On the bears we want to take, rubs aren't a concern.

How much does weather influence the hunt's success or how you hunt in your area?

Wayne Bosowicz: It has a tremendous effect, whether you're hunting with hounds or over bait. When it's raining, you're not going to do anything with hounds. Sometimes if it's just a light mist, or it's just begun, rain will actually increase the scent and help the hounds, but five minutes later, if the rain picks up and washes it out, you're licked. Bait hunting is about the same because the bear lives by its nose. It is true that "what a deer hears, a bear smells, and a wolf sees." Rain makes it tough for bears to determine by smell what's going on around them, and they become incredibly cautious when coming to a bait. When a bear starts smelling around cautiously where a hunter is waiting, it will find people quite a lot of the time when it's raining. So weather, especially rain, is not good for bear hunting. It often doesn't even need to rain; a low-pressure system can have the same effect.

Wade Lemon: Weather plays a pretty big role. Rain can either help you or hurt you. If you can strike a fresh trail early after a rain, your dogs can really trail the bear well. If you get a rain, and you don't find the track until a little later, though, after the rain, and the steam is coming up out of the ground and things are starting to dry out, it seems as though the scent leaves ten times faster. You'd be much better off if it hadn't rained at all. Heavy rain while you're hunting can be a problem, too.

A big Wisconsin bear almost fills the tailgate behind the dog boxes. (Photo courtesy of Jerry Nykanen)

Jerry "Finn" Nykanen: Weather isn't much of a factor, unless it's a real downpour of rain.

Mike Richie: Not a whole lot, unless it's really, really hot. When you get a cold, wet spring, too, it can be slow until the weather improves. Bears don't like to move in cold, wet weather, but once it warms up they move around pretty well. Heat is the main reason we have problems because it's really hard on the dogs. If you get a bear that's running really hard and you don't catch him right away, you're not going to catch him.

Give us your perspective on black bear hunting with hounds as a game management tool.

Wayne Bosowicz: It's the best, and maybe the only, tool we have. That's not so much true of hound hunting because in any state in which hounds are legal the take by that method is only a small percentage of the total kill. Bear hunting in general, and particularly by baiting, is the only way that biologists have to reach their harvest goals—and even with it they still fall short.

The hound people don't take many bears anywhere. We make a big splash because we're highly visible, with several vehicles and radar collars and all, but to take a bear a day with hounds is really tough. With baiting, taking six or seven or more a day is no problem because we do it quietly.

Wade Lemon: Numbers need to be kept in check because bears are really tough on elk and other game animals. I found a cow elk that a bear had killed this year. It had literally ripped her open and dragged out her calf and eaten it. It left the cow to rot and never came back to it. I think that they want fresh meat, and they just kill another elk if they want more. Bears learn by association, and that particular bear is going to teach its offspring to kill elk. Boars will also kill their own young, so you actually preserve the population by killing some of them.

Jerry "Finn" Nykanen: Deer hunters just hate bears. They put out a little corn for the deer, and the black bears come in and immediately eat all their bait. They urge us to kill every single bear, but we go with the state's management regimen and depend on hunters with tags to harvest a bear.

Mike Richie: You've got to manage the bear population if you're going to have any other game. Black bears are the most effective predator of elk and moose calves, as well as deer fawns—or at least they were until we got wolves in the Selway. If you don't hunt the black bears, they can really wipe out the newborns during the fawning and calving periods. The older boars that we want to take are the most efficient at predation, and when we take one out we save a lot of young animals. Last spring we killed quite a few bears, and most had teeth that were green from eating grass and other vegetation. The two biggest boars we killed, though, had perfectly white teeth, which may be an indication that they were eating meat. My wife's brother is a sawyer, and he's in the woods all the time. He actually saw a black bear run down and kill an adult deer two years ago. I've never seen that myself, but I know of several credible people who have.

Section III

HUNTING BY SPOT-AND-STALK

Chapter 12

SELECTING AN OUTFITTER/GUIDE FOR HUNTING BY SPOT-AND-STALK

What should a hunter look for when seeking a black bear outfitter/guide?

Darren DeLuca: I think that the biggest factor in spot-and-stalk hunting is probably the physical condition of the hunter. The hunter must match up the style of the hunt to his physical capabilities. Spot-and-stalk can sometimes be very strenuous, especially getting back into some of the harder areas. However, we do have the ability to adjust our hunts to the hunter's capabilities to a certain extent. For example, we do a lot of hunting from boats, and the stalk might be only a hundred yards or so. Sometimes, though, it's necessary to walk back into a valley for a considerable distance. The hunter has to think, "How do I want to hunt?" A lot of hunters are getting older and don't get around the way they once did. So, in my opinion, matching your physical condition to the nature of the hunt is extremely important.

Mark Galla: It depends to some degree on what the hunter is looking for in the way of a trophy, and also what kind of experience. Game populations would be one thing to research, as well as the size of the animals being taken. One should look at the experience of the outfitter, and what sort of operation and service he provides.

Kevin Olmstead: The hunter first has to decide what type of bear he wants to harvest, and how he wants to hunt it: Is he looking for size, color phase, a baited hunt, spot-and-stalk? One of the big problems is that a lot of hunters aren't sure. Most black bear hunting in North America is done over bait, and there are very few places to do classic spot-and-stalk hunting. Here in British Columbia, it's the only way to do it. Once the

A great coastal Alaska black bear taken with a handgun. (Photo courtesy of Mark Galla)

A big bear taken with a modern firearm in Alaska. (Photo courtesy of Mark Galla)

hunter has decided those things, he can then begin to look at specific outfitters that offer what he's looking for. Next, check references. You need to feel comfortable talking to your guide or outfitter over the phone—but get those references, too, and check with the provincial or state guide and outfitter association. After that it comes down to a gut feeling of who you're most comfortable with.

Another consideration is the cost of the hunt because spot-and-stalk hunting is considerably more expensive than baited hunting, for several reasons. In our type of hunting, we've got to have a guide with the hunter all the time. If you really want to get a big bear, you've got to go somewhere that has them. On some of the less expensive hunts, your odds of killing a truly huge black bear can be pretty small. We are in a two-bear area, but we encourage our hunters to hunt hard until they get that big one. Then, if they want to, they can go out and look for one that's even bigger. So many guys just want to kill something of any size first, and then look for the big one. We discourage that mentality. I tell people who are thinking that way to wait until they're ready to take a really big bear before they come hunting with us. I'd rather see a hunter go home without a bear than kill a small one.

Jimmie Rosenbruch: I think that you look at the same things you want in any guide: experience, references, and his record as a guide. You want to try to go to the right place at the right time with the right people because those are the things a guide can control. He can't control weather and game movement and the like, so look for a guide who's on top of what he can control. You should exercise prudence in selecting a bear guide, just as you would hunting any other species.

What are (a) the most important single characteristic and (b) the worst possible deficiency in a black bear guide?

Darren DeLuca: Without question the worst characteristic in a guide is lack of safety—taking chances on the water, taking chances in the mountains, or taking chances with the animal—and thus putting himself and the hunter in danger. That type of guide is the kind that creates sleepless nights for me, and we just don't keep that kind of guy around. The very best guide is one that keeps everything on an even keel, even when he gets into some kind of bind. You always have some tough situations, dealing with the outdoors the way we do. You need a guide who can keep his head regardless of the hand he's dealt. It's also extremely important that the guide be personable because this is really a people business. A lot of hunters want the best hunting guide they can get, but the best guide might not be the best people person. It's extremely important that guides be personable.

Mark Galla: The most important characteristic is that the guide know his area and the animals in it, as well as their habits. He should also be able to cater to the needs of his hunters and keep his composure in difficult situations, even with difficult people. The worst deficiency would be an inability to interact well with people.

A terrific Vancouver Island trophy black bear. (Photo courtesy of Darren DeLuca)

Kevin Olmstead: I think what's most important is that the guide have good rapport with his clients and know the species he's hunting. The other thing is that he should have as much knowledge of the area as possible; I don't think that's as important as being a good hunter or having a good rapport with the client, though. The worst guide is the one who has no patience and no rapport with the client. When you've got to spend day after day with that guide, and he's not accommodating or sociable, it's going to be a miserable trip. Guided hunting is not just about killing an animal; it's the whole experience. If the guide can't hold up his end of the deal, he's not going to be successful, no matter what kind of animal he helps his client to take.

Jimmie Rosenbruch: The most important characteristic in a guide is being willing to learn. It appears to me that the learning curve tops out for black bear guides about three years into their career. At that point, they think they know everything.

Glassing Vancouver Island amid spectacular scenery.

From then on, though, you find out that you know less and less! The worst characteristic is someone who knows it all—I'd shy away from someone like that, I think. The best guide is someone who's still open, still learning about how it all works, and who has a good track record.

Is there any exceptional qualification for being a black bear guide that may not apply to other types of guiding?

Darren DeLuca: One such qualification is the ability to judge bears. You can pick up judging elk or deer fairly quickly, but bears are different, and you really don't ever know for sure until you put the animal on the ground. And you've got to do a few before you start getting the hang of it. Even with all the bears I've killed with hunters over the years, I still walk up to the animal after we've killed it with my heart in my throat a bit, wondering if I made the right call.

The Rosenbruch bear yacht is a comfortable method of hunting Alaska for bears. (Photo courtesy of Jimmie Rosenbruch)

Mark Galla: I'd say that one of the biggest things is field judging bears for trophy size and determining sex and whether there are cubs present. Those are the most important things a guide has to make decisions on, and often it can become a problem with clients. They can be sitting there wanting to know only if it's a bear big enough to shoot, and in the meantime we're trying to figure out all of the other angles as well. Sometimes it takes a good bit of time to figure it out, and sometimes the animal will even slip away before we can make that determination. We do our utmost to prevent taking a female, even a legal one without cubs, if we can help it. It's illegal to take a sow with cubs, so in every case you've got to be sure none are hidden back in the brush.

Kevin Olmstead: I don't think so. A good guide is a good guide. The reason I say this is that some of my sheep guides come over and help us to hunt black bears in the Queen Charlotte Islands, and they do just fine. A guide who knows how to hunt and who understands the movement of the animals and who is a good companion to his hunter is going to be successful.

Good fishing is one plus for hunting black bears in Alaska. (Photo courtesy of Jimmie Rosenbruch)

Jimmie Rosenbruch: I think that bears are the hardest animal on the planet to judge accurately. There are no horns or antlers to look at, and what you need in a guide is someone who can assess the animal's size and other characteristics. Even today I make mistakes judging the size of bears. That is especially true if you're looking for an exceptional animal, and not just any decent bear. You're not going to kill a big bear by shooting a little one, and you should maintain that standard right through the last day of the hunt. Don't drop your skull size goal by an inch each day into the hunt.

What does a good black bear guide do to ensure safety while hunting a uniquely dangerous animal?

Darren DeLuca: Usually, the mountains and the ocean are far more dangerous than the bear. As regards the bear itself, though, it's making sure that the first shot is a killer. You try to make sure

Alaska black bear hunters take some monster animals. (Photo courtesy of Jimmie Rosenbruch)

that the hunter has a good shot and a good rest, that he's calmed down sufficiently, and so on. The goal is to avoid finding yourself with a wounded bear, which can indeed be dangerous, because you have no idea what's coming. I've been on a lot of hunts for wounded bears. It's always exciting, but it's also stressful—and usually unnecessary. It's especially dangerous with a gut-shot bear because the bear is not really disabled at all; it's capable of doing some damage, and it's very angry.

Mark Galla: That really varies with the hunter's choice of weapon. With a rifle, as opposed to a bow, you're usually at a comfortable range to shoot the animal. It doesn't become an issue unless you have to go into the brush after a wounded animal, which unfortunately happens sometimes. When it does, I'm always the point guy going in, which gives the hunter an extra measure of safety. Another thing is to be aware of your surroundings, and try to pick a vantage point so there is good visibility all around, which in actuality is seldom the case. If an animal happens to come in downwind of you, they don't know you're there, so you've got to be on the alert, paying attention, or they can be right on top of you before you know it. We've actually had very few truly dangerous encounters with black bears, but it's a different story with brown bears.

Kevin Olmstead: What's most important is putting the client in the right position, and looking out for the client while you're hunting. It's not really much different for our black bear guides than our moose and elk guides, because when hunting on the mainland they're often around grizzly bears. Also, it's necessary to know your client's capabilities, both physically and with their weapon, so you can plan ahead.

Jimmie Rosenbruch: I think that the elements and the habitat we hunt are more dangerous than the bear. Clearly, a bear is an animal that is capable of doing some damage to you, but with a good backup from your guide, that shouldn't be a problem. We're very careful in the small skiffs we use to get to the hunting areas, and we use good equipment and a slow, methodical approach. We also pay strict attention to firearm handling, which is more of a hazard than any bear. We have all rifles empty, magazine and all, while we're in the boats. After I tell a guy to chamber a round, he'd better not point that thing at me even once, or we're done!

Chapter 13

SPOT-AND-STALK GUIDES EVALUATE THE HUNTER

What is your favorite type of hunter (personality, physical abilities, experience level, socioeconomic status)?

Darren DeLuca: A good personality is probably what I like most. If a guy can't get around because he's older or handicapped, I certainly don't hold that against him; in fact, I will respect him for having the motivation to get up and go hunting. Whether he's rich or dirt poor really doesn't matter to me. It's about being a good hunting partner more than anything else, and that makes the hunt a pleasure for the guide. You spend a lot of time in the field together, and it really helps to have someone who is personable. What you don't want is someone who's always trying to second-guess you and question your decisions.

Mark Galla: What I certainly enjoy is a hunter who realizes that he's hunting, not buying an animal. Hunting is hunting, and sometimes because of uncontrollable variables it isn't always a slam-dunk. I like a guy who knows that simply because he paid cash up front, it doesn't buy him an animal: It's going to take some hard work and perseverance to get the job done. I especially like someone who's not so focused on killing an animal but who is enjoying being out in the wilderness, enjoying the sights and sounds, and having a good time. That kind of person is going to have a successful hunt whether or not he gets an animal. It seems to me that rich clients are overrated because often the guy with big money has an unrealistic expectation level. The guy who mows lawns on the weekends to get his hunting money often has less demanding expectations than someone who's affluent, in my experience.

Kevin Olmstead: We like a guy who's out there looking for adventure as well as a quality trophy. It's not necessarily

Hunters should come with appropriate clothing, gear, and weapon.

something they will say to you, but you can tell what they're looking for. What's really tough is when a hunter shows up saying that he's looking for a big bear, but then he wants to shoot the first one that comes out. A hunter like that is stuck on killing something, not on trying to do what we want him to do—which is to harvest large, mature boars. It seems to me, though, that 99 percent of the hunters we get today are great people who want to be outdoors and enjoy a hunting adventure.

Jimmie Rosenbruch: I like the guy who doesn't know it all. We can be very successful with hunters if they'll let us work with them. If you go to see your doctor, your accountant, or your attorney, you're paying them big bucks for what they do for you. It's not much different when you've hired a guide, except that most hunters do know something about hunting because they have some experience with it.

The worst possible hunter, in my opinion, is someone who is of European descent who's hunted everywhere but North America. Frankly, we don't take those kinds of hunters anymore. They simply won't listen, so they don't do very well hunting bears. A woman hunter who's familiar with her firearm is quite a good hunter because she'll listen to what you say and do what you advise her to do. I really like someone who's easygoing because a hunter like that will really enjoy hunting these temperate rain forests, which are different from anywhere else on the planet.

Should inexperienced and physically challenged hunters go hunting for black bears? Why or why not?

Darren DeLuca: I think it's OK for them to go, but I do think that they should limit their expectations somewhat as to what the hunt may accomplish for them. However, a lot of times an inexperienced hunter will take the biggest bear and have the best hunt because hunters like that will listen to their guides and do exactly what they're told. The handicapped hunter also has an issue of expectations, but most guys who are physically limited do recognize and respect that fact.

Most trophy Alaska black bears are taken on coastal flats near thick cover. (Photo courtesy of Mark Galla)

Mark Galla: As for me, I have no problem taking either kind of hunter. The spring hunts are less physically demanding than the fall hunts, so they're ideal for the handicapped hunter. If they can get from the big boat into a skiff, they're good to go in the spring because it's not usually a difficult hunt. As far as experience goes, we've taken teenagers and people in their late eighties. We do what's necessary to give them a chance at a bear, even if it means more work for us, and we don't hesitate to change gears if what we're doing isn't working. We work within the limits of what a hunter is able to do.

Kevin Olmstead: Inexperience is no problem, but physically challenged hunters can be. In spot-and-stalk hunting their ability to hunt is more limited than in bait hunting. We can take handicapped hunters on some of our logging roads where there are big clear-cuts to glass. We welcome those types of hunters, but they need to realize that we're going to the bears, not the other way around. Anytime you're spot-and-stalk hunting, you're at a big disadvantage if you don't have mobility.

Jimmie Rosenbruch: Absolutely. The broader the base we can create for hunting bears, the better off we are. Sometimes it takes a little special effort, but the state of Alaska allows a handicapped hunter to shoot from a skiff. We've even had quadriplegics be successful in taking bears. As far as inexperience, we were all inexperienced at one time, so that's not usually a problem.

Is there any particular characteristic in a hunter that would make you refuse to guide him on a black bear hunt ?

Darren DeLuca: I'd refuse to guide any hunter who is careless or unsafe with a firearm. In my contract I have included a clause which states that if a hunter refuses to follow instructions in matters of safety, the hunt is over; I refund the balance remaining on the hunt. The hunt is meant to be enjoyable, but everybody should be able to look forward to getting home safely.

Mark Galla: Certainly I'd refuse to guide anyone who wanted to do the hunt by unethical means. I haven't much patience with people who aren't there to hunt ethically and by the book. Also, while I won't necessarily refuse to guide them, some guys want to bring a gun that's just not adequate for the size of bear we're hunting here in southeast Alaska. There are certainly some things that you can't know until the client is in camp, such as an alcohol or drug habit. I have no issue with a person having a drink after we're done for the day and we're back in camp, as long as there's no getting out of control. But I won't put up with alcohol in the field while we're hunting.

Kevin Olmstead: It's not just black bear hunters: Among all hunters you do get the odd guy who simply won't listen. The hunter has hired us to do a job for him, and we take whatever information the hunter gives us and learn from it. But that goes both ways—the hunter's got to learn from us, too. If you get a hunter who's not safety-oriented and won't listen to the guide, that would be someone I'd be reluctant to have back.

Contemplating heading out on foot after a bear. (Photo courtesy of Jimmie Rosenbruch)

Another problem would be the hunter who refuses to abide by established governmental regulations. We're looking for real sportsmen as our clients, people who will only take a shot that they feel comfortable they can make and that will result in a clean and humane kill.

Jimmie Rosenbruch: If a guy walks up to our booth at a convention and he's got earrings and a necklace, and he's been bending his arm a little more than he should, we don't like to take him. And I won't take someone if I know he's an attorney! We also avoid know-it-alls, party animals, and the like. We're usually booked out a couple of years, so we can afford to be choosy. We don't normally use any booking agents, so we're able to be a bit selective. We're on a boat, and we have to live, eat, and sleep with these hunters for days on end. We have a great time and make good friends 99.9 percent of the

Leaving the big boat heading for the hunting grounds. (Photo courtesy of Jimmie Rosenbruch)

time, and it's a fabulous experience. We keep that ratio high by being a bit selective in whom we take hunting.

What is the most dangerous thing a client can do while hunting black bears? Can you share an instance in which a client placed himself (or the guide) in danger?

Darren DeLuca: An extremely dangerous situation occurs when you're on a stalk and the guide tells the client to put a round in the chamber, and the hunter walks along with the rifle pointed right at the guide's back. This is, unfortunately, very common. For that reason, we tell the hunter to put a shell in the chamber only when he's actually in shooting position. Another thing that's dangerous is when guys show up with guns that are so big they think that they can hit the bear anywhere and it will die. They think they can shoot the bear in the butt with a .375 and kill it, just because the gun's big. Often, though, the caliber is much too heavy for them to

A trophy Alaska black bear, the result of a successful stalk. (Photo courtesy of Jimmie Rosenbruch)

handle well; they're a little afraid of it and make poor shots. Then we've got a wounded bear on our hands, and we have to go out there and sort it out.

Mark Galla: Without question the most dangerous thing a hunter can do is handle a firearm in an unsafe manner. In more than one instance I've had clients whose guns have gone off accidentally. Fortunately there's never been any damage done. Of course, it's always the fault of the gun! Bowhunting is inherently more dangerous because the animal is so close. If he knows where the hunter is located and feels the sting of the hit, the bear may come looking for you. Getting between a mother bear and her cubs is, of course, dangerous, but we carefully avoid doing that, and it's never happened.

Kevin Olmstead: Firearm safety is most important to me. I'm not talking about taking a shot and maybe not getting the best hit, and then having to go in after the bear. That's going to happen from time to time, despite our best efforts. I'm talking about the guy who is simply not safe with a firearm, not knowing when to load and when to unload, or where to point it.

Jimmie Rosenbruch: We run quite an orientation before we start hunting. We have our clients sit still after the shot. We don't want them up moving around until we've had time to listen, to determine if the bear is moving. It's important not to race up immediately to try to see what's happening. You need to sit still after the shot and assess. Partly it's because the bear has the capacity to be dangerous, but on a more practical level, you want to see how effective the shot was, and where the bear goes afterward. In all our years of guiding, I can't recall a single episode in which something dangerous has happened because we always try to do the right thing after the shot. Sometimes the bear will run toward you and it looks like a charge, but usually they're heading for the closest cover. Frankly, the most dangerous possibility is the client shooting the guide, which is far more dangerous than any encounter with a bear.

Chapter 14

SPOT-AND-STALK GUIDES EVALUATE HUNTING ARMS

What is your favorite rifle caliber for black bears, and do you recommend this caliber for clients?

Darren DeLuca: I shoot a .338. I feel that it has enough knockdown at close range if we're going in on a wounded bear, but it's also able to reach out two hundred yards if we need to do that. It offers the best of both worlds. It also comes with some pretty heavy bullets, too, and I can shoot 225-grain or 250-grain. For hunters, I like to see a minimum of a .30-06 shooting 180-grain bullets, but I'd rather see them using 200-grain bullets. I'll bend that rule a little bit for smaller hunters—women, kids, and so on. Calibers I don't like are 7mm and .270. Here on the island we do a lot of shooting between thirty and fifty yards, and the bullet is just moving much too fast to get any kind of expansion. As a result, the bullet goes right through the bear, leaving a very small hole and a very minimal blood trail—and another tough job following up on a wounded bear.

Mark Galla: In my opinion, you're just not going to overgun one of our Alaska bears. We're not shooting 150- to 200-pound bears; we're shooting 350- to 600-pound bears, and the black bear is a tough animal. The shock of the bullet hitting doesn't stop a bear, so what you have to do is break them down and shut them down with proper shot placement. What I tell guys who want to bring some little peashooter of a gun is to go ahead and bring it, and after they've riled the bear up I'll kill it for them.

Kevin Olmstead: Anything .30 caliber or bigger is good, but I don't stress that so much because I want them to use a gun they shoot well. Ideally, everyone would use a .300 magnum, but if they've been using a .270 and they have absolute confidence in their ability with it, I'd rather they be shooting that one. They

Bow kill in dense cover in Alaska. (Photo courtesy of Mark Galla)

need to be able to do good bullet placement more than anything else, and they can't do that if they're afraid of the rifle.

Jimmie Rosenbruch: We don't like our clients to use less than a .375. We're hunting black bears that are the size of grizzly bears, and these small calibers just don't do the job. I once had a lady client from Mexico who shot a bear with a 7mm, and I extracted the bullet out of the bear's toe. Don't ask me how that happened. For us, the .375 is the minimum, the .416 is ideal, and we even like to see .458s.

What is your choice as a backup weapon when guiding for black bears?

Darren DeLuca: The .338. Mine is a Remington 700 BDL. A lot of guys take shotguns or other close-in type weapons, but the problem with that comes when you're tracking the bear and you suddenly see him out at 50 yards and moving away. What do you do then if you're carrying a shotgun with buckshot? He's already out of range! The .338 gives me the flexibility I need for any situation.

Mark Galla: I use a .375 H&H.

Kevin Olmstead: Most of our guides carry a .300 or .338.

Jimmie Rosenbruch: The whole crew uses either a .416 or a .458.

What is your advice on bullet weight? Bullet construction?

Darren DeLuca: I like Nosler Partition bullets. When I was guiding a lot, I shot Federal Premiums most of the time, but I've sort of moved over to the Winchester Fail Safes now. I still use both.

Mark Galla: I lean toward the heaviest bullet made for the caliber. We're not out there shooting great distances, and we strive to make all our shots one hundred yards or less. A slightly lighter bullet that will reach out a little farther isn't much of an advantage most of the time. As far as bullet construction, I like the Barnes X-Bullet, Trophy Bonded Bear Claw, and Fail Safe. Any of the heavier bonded bullets are good. I know there are various opinions on the Nosler Partition bullet, but my experience with them has been good, so I consider them a good option as well.

Big bear taken in Alaska with a modern rifle. (Photo courtesy of Mark Galla)

Kevin Olmstead: I'm not really a ballistics guy, but in a .30 caliber I recommend at least a 180-grain bullet, and in something like a Nosler Partition, something that retains its weight. You need a heavier bullet that holds together.

Jimmie Rosenbruch: We tell our clients to buy the heaviest expanding round-nosed bullets their gun will shoot well. What doesn't work well is the Noslers, or any of the partition-type bullets. Bears have soft skin, and if you shoot a small hole in and a small hole out, you'll have problems.

Do you have any tips on shooting techniques in field situations ?

Darren DeLuca: I really don't particularly, other than the standard "get a rest." That's the primary concern, so you can make sure the first shot is a good, clean one. Also, it's my practice always to have my scope turned to the lowest possible power, so I have the largest available field of view. Then if there's a need to dial it up a bit, there's usually plenty of time. If you've got it dialed up to the point that you've got a poor field of view, you may not even be able to find the animal.

Mark Galla: One thing I try to get people to do before they arrive is to practice in field situations. So many guys go out and crank off a few rounds off the bench and think that they're ready to hunt. They need to do some offhand shooting and some shooting from odd positions, such as sitting. It's good to be able to make the shot from different ranges and under different conditions.

Kevin Olmstead: The main thing is to be calm and to try to get a rest for the rifle. We tell our hunters to put the bullet in the little V that's right behind the shoulder. If we're in really thick cover where we need to put that bear down as quickly as possible, I have them go for the shoulder. It's very important that a hunter not take a shot if he's not comfortable and sure he can make it.

Jimmie Rosenbruch: Yes, I can offer some tips. We cripple and lose a few bears, and that's a shame. In most places in the

Competent handgun hunters can kill huge black bears. (Photo courtesy of Mark Galla)

world, if you wound an animal and lose it, the hunt's over. Alaska now has a law that does essentially that for bears. If you wound a bear in the southeastern Alaska rain forest, your hunt's over. It's a good rule, too. Bears don't leave tracks and don't bleed very much, so they can get away wounded. My tip on field shooting is to do it very carefully, so you don't lose a wounded bear.

What advice do you give your hunters on shot placement on a black bear?

Darren DeLuca: We recommend that the hunter try for a heart-lung shot and try to take out a shoulder as the shot exits. That way we can often knock them down so we can get another shot ready and get it off. If you get a heart-lung shot and it goes straight through, the bear usually runs off and you don't know if you've hit him or not. On these spot-and-stalk hunts you're usually watching the bear ambling around, and he's not going anywhere, so you have time to be patient and wait for exactly the right position for the shot. Here on Vancouver Island, at least, there's always another bear, so don't hurry it and mess up the shot. If you do, you've got a wounded bear to deal with. Then you're going to lose at least that day of hunting, and you're going to feel bad about yourself and about the hunt. So be patient and wait for a good broadside shot.

Mark Galla: The perfect shot is broadside through the center of the shoulders, which will take out both shoulders and the heart and lungs in between. The main thing is to break them down in the front. If the hunter does that, we'll recover the bear. Any shot outside that area causes the loss rate to skyrocket, and we may not find it.

Kevin Olmstead: I prefer that the hunter put the shot right behind the shoulder, so it's a heart-lung shot, or right through the shoulder to get both the heart and lungs and take out a shoulder at the same time.

Jimmie Rosenbruch: The bottom line is that you need to shoot your bear very carefully, and it's got to be a heart-lung shot. Broken legs won't slow them down, but a good shot through the lungs will take the bear. Breaking a shoulder isn't nearly as important as hitting the vitals. The basis of the new Alaska law is that if the bear is hit, you've killed it, whether or not you recover it. But if you don't hit it well, you won't recover it. Make a good shot in the heart-lung area, and we'll find that bear, even in the dense cover where they usually run.

How many of your first-time black bear hunters are intimidated by the prospect of hunting a dangerous animal? Describe some typical reactions.

Darren DeLuca: I don't recommend that you go out and buy a bear attack book right before you come! Guys hunting black bears are usually pretty well prepared mentally, so they're not too intimidated. People from Europe don't do much bear hunting, though, so it seems that they're a little more stressed out about it. Most North American hunters handle it pretty well and are comfortable hunting black bears.

Mom and cub watch hunters warily on Vancouver Island. (Photo courtesy of Darren DeLuca)

Mark Galla: Frankly, I've not had that much of an issue with hunters being intimidated. Again, though, we strive to make sure that our hunters don't get overexcited. We keep things calm, get them set up, and usually the bear has no idea we're in the area.

Kevin Olmstead: It's a smaller percentage than you might think who are intimidated. There may be some element of apprehension when they first arrive because nobody's really talked to them about how the hunt might go. But by the time we've gone over shot placement and what to expect, they become much more comfortable. Good communication with the client does a lot to allay anxiety. Most of the time it's not a fear factor, though; it's just the normal and expected excitement we all feel before a big hunt—and it's one of the main reasons people hunt. If we completely lost that feeling of exhilaration, many of us would probably quit hunting!

A great Vancouver Island black bear. (Photo courtesy of Darren DeLuca)

Jimmie Rosenbruch: I find that there's usually a little apprehension, but it actually adds to the enjoyment and anticipation of the hunt. I don't know that everybody is intimidated the first time, but I think that a concern for personal safety is always there. We sometimes have very close encounters, particularly in the fall, and the bear can walk by within a few yards and never know we're there. The hunter gets a little nervous when that happens, and I really watch for their reaction. I always have the client shoot on the beach before we go hunting because I want to know how he handles his gun.

How do you prepare for and handle overpowering excitement in a hunter/client?

Darren DeLuca: We show the hunter a few bears and let him get over some of his excitement. If a guy wants to shoot the first bear he sees, he doesn't have time to get acclimated, so to speak. If we can show him some bears and maybe do a few practice stalks, it seems to help a lot. If I see a guy starting to hyperventilate, we just sit tight until the excitement subsides a little and the heart rate comes back to normal. I also watch them very carefully and don't let them load their gun prematurely. I try to walk them through it, but if there's still a problem, we'll pull off that bear and maybe try again the next day.

Mark Galla: I've had a handful get uncontrollably excited, and we usually work it out. If a guy starts shaking, we generally take a time out and try to calm him down before we'll let him take a shot. In some cases it costs us the chance to take that particular animal, but on the other hand you don't want somebody pulling the trigger when he's that excited. You'll probably end up worse off than if he hadn't taken the shot at all.

Kevin Olmstead: You just have to talk to them. Some hunters get so excited they couldn't hit the broad side of a barn. Most of the time when a hunter either makes too much noise and blows the stalk, or misses a shot because of excitement, you just sit down and talk to him. You don't get upset; you just talk it out. Then the next time you get into that situation, you know that you've got to start a little earlier keeping the hunter calm, and the hunter knows a lot more about what to expect. So much of it is communication with your client, because so many of them are doing something they've never done before.

Jimmie Rosenbruch: We talk to them continuously. I always get positioned close to the hunter so we can converse. I'm always saying, "Not yet, not yet. Wait. He's facing away from you; don't shoot. He's turned now, shoot!" The hunter has to be the one to decide exactly when to shoot, though, and if he's getting that good window he needs to touch it off. Often there's only a ten-second window to get the job done in, and if you don't pull it off then, you might not get another opportunity because that bear's gone. Our entire staff is trained to keep up a constant dialogue with the client so that he won't be so excited he misses that ten-second window. I can often get a better idea if it's a hit by watching the client shoot than by watching the bear.

Could you take this black bear without a modern rifle? (Photo courtesy of Jimmie Rosenbruch)

If a hunter is really nervous, the result is poor shot placement. But we try our best to minimize that.

Do you have any wise words on bowhunting? Black-powder hunting?

Darren DeLuca: Black-powder hunting these days is pretty much rifle hunting. Most of our shooting is between forty and fifty yards, so it's ideal for black powder. We do have some problems with moisture, though. The big thing with both bowhunting and black powder is that you're basically shooting a single shot, and that's a limiting factor. The first shot has got to be good. We have a rule on both bowhunting and black-powder hunting, that if we judge that the shot is a killing shot we let the bear run off and die. If the shot is too far back or otherwise misplaced, we have to use the backup weapon so we don't lose the bear. Bow hunters can be pretty upset if you use the rifle on their bears because it disqualifies them for Pope and Young. But we explain ahead of time our criteria for shooting. Even if a guy makes a good shot and the bear runs off, he knows ahead of time that the bear is his—even if we can't find it. They can't come up here and shoot four or five bears trying to take one home. With bow hunters it's practice, practice, practice. Be prepared for a shot at a bear that's not forty yards away sitting still on the lawn. Here you're going to have a shot at a bear either above or below you, so practice those kinds of shots. Be ready, because the bear you find here will not act like a target-practice bear.

Mark Galla: We take both types of hunter, and I have no problem working with either. Black-powder hunting is hardly even a handicap anymore, except that we're working with only a single shot. The main thing is to get the client set up really well so that he gets a good, solid hit. We don't want our bow hunters taking shots at more than twenty-five to thirty yards. We had a hunter last fall miss an excellent bear at thirty yards in failing light, when he tried a head-on shot and, naturally, missed. He thought that the bear was turned a little more than it actually was. All he'd had to do was wait and that bear would have walked right out in front of us. But he got overeager and it cost him a great trophy.

Again, anytime you're going to fling an arrow at a dangerous animal, if that animal knows you're there, he may come looking for you. The bow hunter should be ready to pass on a shot if everything isn't ideal. I had one hunter who was talking about trying to make a femoral artery shot, and man, that's crazy, when you consider the size of the artery you're trying to hit! A double lung shot with a bow is a lethal shot on a bear, and no other kind should be attempted. You're taking a big chance at wounding and losing the animal otherwise. Alaska regulations now define a wounded bear as a dead bear, so if you wound and lose a bear, your hunt's over.

Kevin Olmstead: We take some bow hunters, and we enjoy working with them. With these weapons you have to stalk a little closer and get good shot placement. So far we haven't had a black-powder hunter in the Queen Charlottes, but we would have no reason to turn them down. It's very wet up here, but the in-line muzzleloaders are so moisture-proof that they shouldn't have a problem with the rain.

Jimmie Rosenbruch: No, we don't do either. For a long time they didn't allow bowhunting in southeastern Alaska because following the bear after it's hit is such a difficult task. As for black powder, we have so much wet weather here that it's literally hard to keep your powder dry, so it's not the ideal place for that, either.

Do you take any special precautions when hunting with bow hunters or black-powder hunters?

Darren DeLuca: If we judge they've made a good shot, we let the bear run off to die. If we see an arrow or bullet wound in the butt or guts, it's more than a precaution. It's our responsibility to shoot. We make certain that our bow hunters and black-powder hunters understand this up front, so there's no surprise. If they can't live with that—well, they'll have to hunt with somebody else. We don't want anybody to get hurt, and we sure don't want any bear running around with an arrow stuck in its rear.

Mark Galla: As for black-powder hunters, there isn't a lot of difference between them and regular rifle hunters. We try to get within one hundred yards with either kind of firearm. With a bow, you get to within thirty yards or so, and then my big concern is whether the bear is aware of your presence. As I've said, if they are, they might head right for you when they get hurt. Most bow hunters have hunted a lot of ungulates, which won't come after you when they're shot, and they may not be aware that shooting a bear when it's looking right at you isn't a very good idea. Of course, I'm always there to back the hunter up.

Kevin Olmstead: We do it exactly the same, as far as the actual hunting is concerned.

Chapter 15

HUNTING BLACK BEARS BY SPOT-AND-STALK

What is the most common mistake made by guided black bear hunters?

Darren DeLuca: I don't know that there's a most common mistake, but if there is it's probably misjudging the size of the bear. Sometimes hunters think all of them are monsters. You've really got to trust the judgment of the guide, but keep in mind that he's not infallible. He's far more trustworthy than the hunter, though, who's not even familiar with the rain forest where we hunt. A lot of times hunters make the mistake of trying to push the guide, trying to get him to let them shoot a bear because the hunter thinks it's big, or pushing the guide to stay out late on the water in a boat. We like to have everyone off the water by dark. Sometimes you can get into a dangerous situation by staying just a little longer—often at the urging of the hunter. The guides know better, but every once in a while they get talked into it and it turns into a disaster. Again, it all comes from not listening to the guide, whose job it is to get you a good bear and get you home safely.

Mark Galla: Making noise is a big mistake. It seems that so many hunters just can't move quietly through the brush, and that can be difficult at times, I admit. A lot of hunters simply don't seem to understand the concept of being stealthy. Also, a big percentage of hunters approach shooting a bear as if they were shooting a deer or elk. They shoot the animal, it falls down, and that's that. I hammer this message into my hunters: When you shoot at a bear, you put another shot in it immediately. You don't stop and admire the beautiful shot you just made, and you don't lay down your gun and assume it's all over. Put another shot into the bear! Some 90 percent of the time a bear is going

Hunters should help guides find and evaluate signs of bear activity.

to get up and run—if it falls down at all. The biggest problem I have is guys who make a good shot, the bear goes down and does a couple of spins, and the hunter lowers his gun to admire his work. All of a sudden that bear's up and running at thirty-five miles per hour, and the client has just lost the opportunity to get another round into the animal. I've never once had a black bear run into the brush and lie down to wait for me to come after him—although brown bears do it regularly, and blacks do, too, on occasion. Get in that second or third shot so you don't wind up tracking your bear through the thicket.

Kevin Olmstead: Size judgment can be a big problem when you're looking at a bear. Hunters often don't listen to their guide, but they need to trust his judgment and not try to make their own decision. When they start to question the judgment of their guide, they're making a big mistake.

Jimmie Rosenbruch: It's common for the hunter to think that it's "just a black bear" and become complacent about shot placement, the stalk, and so on. These big bears have been around awhile, and it's not their first rodeo. They live in a world that for the most part is absolutely silent; the least bit of unusual noise, and they're out of there. And it's a myth that bears can't see because they see at least as well as a human. They've got ears like a whitetail, a nose like only bears have, and they see well. If the bear detects you, it's gone, so you need to be quiet, move into the wind, and stay out of sight. The guide can keep you downwind and out of sight, but he can't completely control it when his hunter is making noise; that's the number one mistake. The first day out in the field, we make every necessary modification to boots and equipment to keep the noise down.

What can a guided hunter do that would most improve his chances of success (patience, physical fitness, mental preparation, equipment, practice with choice of weapon)?

Darren DeLuca: All of the above, plus giving themselves a chance to learn the area and how we hunt here. If they've been on a bait hunt, they may have their own ideas about how to hunt bear, and we probably do it entirely differently. It's important, when in Rome, to do as the Romans. The hunter has to let us do our job, both as outfitter and as guide.

Mark Galla: All of the things listed apply, of course. One of the biggest rubs I have with many clients is that they tend not to participate in the hunt. We often cruise the shoreline,

Dominant Vancouver Island boars often bite and break small trees to mark their territory.

and everybody, even the cook, is glassing for bears. I look over and the hunter is sitting on a chair looking at a magazine, or at his toes! This is something they should be participating in! Almost nothing irks me as much as a hunter who just sits there and waits for a tap on the shoulder. What happens is that eventually everyone else tends to lose interest, too, because this guy doesn't seem to care if he finds a bear or not. Participating in the hunt, whether it's glassing, looking at sign, just paying attention to what's going on around you—all these things are what make a hunt.

Kevin Olmstead: Communicating and listening to the guide are by far the most important factors in improving the hunter's chances of success. That's why they have a guide, and it really doesn't matter if you're hunting black bears or moose. The guide is out there to do the best job he can for the client. Guides are human and they make mistakes, too, but 99 percent of the time the guide is doing what he thinks is best for you, the client hunter. It's just not smart to second-guess him.

Jimmie Rosenbruch: You've named all the elements that will improve a hunter's chances, but I don't know that there's any one of them that's more important than the others. You've just got to be completely prepared overall. We send out an equipment list, and it's really not a very long one. Everything on it needs to be brought with you because if it's on the list, you're going to want it. Even if some hunters are not hunting these big black bears we have in southeastern Alaska, they owe it to any animal they're going after to be prepared to do the hunt well and make a clean kill. They need to think about the hunt long before it's time to go to the airport because they owe it to themselves to be prepared so they can fully enjoy the experience.

Besides the weapon, what kind of equipment should every hunter carry? Also, besides the weapon, what is the most important single piece of equipment?

Darren DeLuca: As a safety issue, I'd say that you'd want to have some very basic survival gear, such as matches and a compass. As far as the actual hunting is concerned, good binoculars are important, with a minimum of 8X and a 40mm objective. Those are important because you're often glassing long distances in failing light.

Mark Galla: On our hunts, the most important single piece of equipment would be breathable chest waders. I also like to see quality equipment, not the cheapest you can buy. There's hardly anything worse than having equipment fail when you are out in the middle of nowhere and need it most. Your comfort level goes down dramatically when your cheap boots develop a hole the size of a softball. I'd rate quality optics, including the riflescope, very high on the list, too. I've seen guys come to camp with a gun that cost thousands of dollars and a forty-dollar scope! The weather will definitely apply the quality test to your optical equipment, especially here in southeastern Alaska. Your hunting equipment, including the weapon, should be able to stand being in the shower with the water turned on full bore. If it can't, you need different equipment.

Kevin Olmstead: In our part of the world, nothing comes close to really good rain gear. You've got to be able to stay dry in order to be comfortable and enjoy the hunt, so excellent rain gear is an absolute necessity. The next priority would be good binoculars.

Jimmie Rosenbruch: There are probably several that are important, and I don't know if one is any more important than the others. In our bear hunting, you're always going to be coming back in the dark, so you need a light. It's going to rain, so you need really good rain gear, not synthetic, scratchy, leaky rainwear. It has to be rubberized so it's perfectly dry inside. You need hip boots, too. It comes down to being able to see in order to get home, and also have good protection from the elements.

Are there any common items of equipment that you feel are unnecessary, redundant, or just plain worthless for hunting black bears by spot-and-stalk?

Darren DeLuca: A lot of rifle hunters wear far more camouflage than they need. Bears have poor eyesight compared with ungulates and are much more likely to see motion than shape, particularly at longer distances. You don't have to be totally camouflaged from top to bottom to hunt black bears. It's OK, of course, but it's not a necessity. Watches with alarms and cell phones that ring should be left at home! We're not big on antiscent stuff, either, because if the wind's blowing the wrong way, you're pretty much busted on that bear.

Outfitter Dave Fyfe using a predator call to attract Vancouver Island black bears.

Mark Galla: Spotting scopes aren't needed in our camps. For one thing we already have them, and for another we're moving around in boats a lot of the time, so it's not stable enough to use them. Rangefinders aren't usually needed, either, although I always have one with me. Gore-Tex gloves aren't needed in our area because they always get a thousand needle holes in them and invariably leak. Another item I'd recommend against is anything made of cotton. Cotton gets wet easily and won't dry out very readily, and it makes you colder when it's wet. I tend toward the synthetics instead.

Kevin Olmstead: We supply a really good equipment list, and most of our clients adhere to it pretty well. We limit their weight for flying in, and that helps hold down the amount of unnecessary gear. Some of the weightiest items these days have to do with camera equipment, and that's OK, but as far as unnecessary gear goes, we have a minimum of it.

Jimmie Rosenbruch: Hunters don't need a spotting scope here. In the spring you can bring binoculars, but for our fall hunts you need to leave your binoculars on the boat. You need to be

Hunting coastal rain forest in Alaska for black bears. (Photo courtesy of Jimmie Rosenbruch)

looking at the bear through the riflescope. As I said before, you may have only a ten-second window in which to kill the bear, and when we see a bear you need to be prepared. If you eat up seven or eight seconds of your time looking through binoculars, you don't have time to switch to your rifle. Some guys come with a truckload of trinkets, and we help them cull out the things that aren't necessary. The unneeded items stay on the boat.

Tell us your method of field judging black bears for size.

Darren DeLuca: With the island black bears, the males have a very blocky head. You can see the same thing in Labrador retrievers, where the female dog has a much longer, slimmer head and the males are blocky. It's the same with our bears. I also use the ear characteristics, with at least three ear widths between the ears. The size of the forearm is important, and it should be the same width at the pad in a big boar. If the forearm narrows down at the wrist, it's probably a sow. An older bear will tend to have his front pads turn in and his elbows turn out.

How the animal moves is another factor. A big bear ambles and waddles, and seems to move more slowly, although they may cover a lot of ground. A small bear jumps from stump to stump and log to log, moving quite quickly. One thing I would note is that it's very difficult to judge a bear that's located uphill from you. I just avoid shooting at them, because when they're looking down at you from above they all look like they've got a huge head, they're all pigeon-toed, and so on. It's too easy to make a mistake.

Mark Galla: One of the big indicators is the size of the ears. A smaller bear has ears that seem to be more pronounced. I'm told the ears don't grow much as a bear matures, though I can't personally confirm that. The bigger the head, the more the ears tend to be off to the side. If the ears are standing up like an alert puppy's, chances are that's not going to be a big bear. So the ears are important. The actions of the bear are also revealing because big bears don't waste any movements. They tend to be extremely deliberate, with no quick moves and no flitting around like a cub or a young bear. If you see that, odds are it's a small bear. A big bear also walks differently, in a kind of amble rather than a brisk walk. The bigger they get, the more pigeon-toed they are, and that's another indication it's a big bear. I also look at the size of the nose because big bears seem to have a big nose. If you get a chance to look at their tracks, that's the most tried and true indication, though it's one we rarely get a chance to use. Another thing you can use is the size of objects around the bear, such as boulders or trees, if you have a good indication of how big those are. We have to piece it all together and make a judgment, and it's not perfect no matter how hard you work at it because you're not dealing with an animal with horns.

Kevin Olmstead: I've got some guides who are world experts at judging black bear size, and I'd like to turn this question over to one of them. There are standard parameters they use, but I really don't do that much hands-on guiding anymore; I'd defer to the wisdom of the people in the field with the hunters. I can tell you it's a difficult task, and it could be compared to looking through binoculars at a man a couple of hundred yards away and trying to tell if he's big or little, tall or short.

Jimmie Rosenbruch: It's beyond question the hardest job for anyone hunting black bears. We could do the entire interview on field judging black bears. There are a host of elements, perhaps up to fifty different factors, that you need to look at when sizing up a black bear. Ear size is a classic method of determining how big the bear is, but you've got to be careful and look at everything. What it takes is plenty of time to look the bear over in order to be certain. A big male bear is just big all over. There are face characteristics that are only in the males, and we try to pick those out. The nose of a male is heavier, there's more flesh above the nostrils, and the head is blockier.

What is the most reliable way to determine sex when no cubs are present? Give us some other methods as well.

Darren DeLuca: The blocky head on males, and the narrow wrists on females, are the best indicators.

Mark Galla: The nose on a sow is usually a lot thinner than on a boar. Also, a boar seems to have more of a scowl in the face. The boar will have a squarer, blockier head as well. Of course, if you can see the genitals, which often we can, you can be certain. From time to time a really big, solitary sow will fool us, though, despite every effort we make to avoid taking females.

Kevin Olmstead: In both black and grizzly bears, the head features are most important in determining sex if there are no cubs present.

Jimmie Rosenbruch: We're quite sensitive about sex, but sometimes it's simply impossible to tell the difference, particularly in the fall. A big, dry sow will take on all the proportions of a large male, and you just can't tell. The light's low, there are no cubs around, and occasionally we end up decking a sow. It's something we hate, but it happens. In most cases, though, it's avoidable. A sow tapers from the back to the front much more than a male bear, so she's always more narrow in the shoulders

A big Alaska coastal black bear. (Photo courtesy of Jimmie Rosenbruch)

than she is in the rear, and her neck isn't as long. Still, the only absolute method is seeing penis sheath hair or vagina hair, if the animal turns just right and the light is adequate.

We try not to shoot anything less than eight feet in size, and sometimes we pass up eight-foot black bears because we simply can't tell the sex. Remember, too, that cubs don't always stick close to their mom, so you've really got to be careful. Fortunately, we've never shot a sow with cubs, but I'll tell you, sometimes we've come awfully close, especially in the fall. In the fall it's much more difficult to tell sex because all the bears are heavier then. Sex characteristics are obscured in fall, the cubs don't stay as close as in the spring, and in the fall we're hunting up creeks into the rain forests, and you don't have nearly as much time to look.

How do you normally proceed to follow up after the shot at a black bear?

Darren DeLuca: It depends on the shot, I guess. If the bear is hit and knocked down, we instruct the hunter to keep the bear

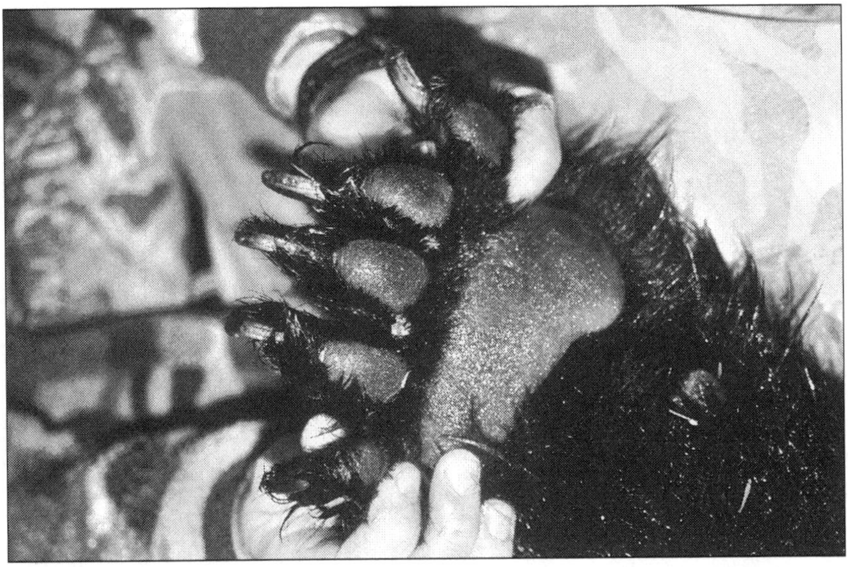

Big paw on a trophy black bear.

in the scope and be ready for a second shot. If he doesn't get up, you still need to be ready. Most bears take two shots, so stay on him until you're sure he isn't getting up. If he does start crawling off, in our kind of country a bear could get just fifty yards or so and we might not be able to recover it. We want that bear dead on the ground, so knock it down and keep it down. I've got a little trick that I wouldn't recommend for others if the bear disappears. After the shot I stay above where I think the bear is, and I generally try to get in there quickly so that I can try to see or hear something. I push the bear a little so it moves, because if it dies in some of the places we hunt, you might never find it, even if it's dead. I want to see movement or hear it thrashing. This trick is a little dangerous, so I don't recommend it for others, but in our country it seems to be the best way to get a bead on where the bear is before it dies.

Mark Galla: Generally we try very hard not to shoot the hunter's animal after the hunter shoots. I wait and let the hunter get off the second shot if at all possible. Frankly, I can't tell you how many times I've been bitten by doing that, but it's the way we operate. If the bear is right on the edge of cover, and I judge that my hunter doesn't have the ability to get off another shot, I generally will do a follow-up shot of my own, rather than risk letting the bear get away wounded. The only exception is if the bear goes right down and doesn't move. However, on more than one occasion we've shot bears that went down immediately, and we thought they were done. But then up they jump and run off; we've even lost bears that way. I had one lady hunter who put a really good shot on a bear that was on the beach, pretty far from cover, and she shot it again as it moved toward the brush. It was literally dragging itself along, and I hesitated to shoot because it appeared to be fatally wounded. I finally decided just to make sure, so I fired just as it reached cover. Five of us looked for many hours trying to locate that bear, and we never did find it. So pretty much don't stop shooting until the bear disappears, or it stops moving completely, or you're out of bullets.

Kevin Olmstead: Our guides always go in first following a shot. If there's thick cover close by, we decide ahead of time with the client whether to put in a backup shot. Depending on the weather conditions, we try to wait for thirty minutes or so before going in after the bear, to give the animal time to either stiffen up a bit or die. With so much rain, we often have to go immediately and try to follow the trail. If it's a day with no rain we wait a while, but if it's raining hard we go after the animal right away.

Jimmie Rosenbruch: As I mentioned before, our routine is to sit tight and see what's going to happen. We also explain to our hunters before we go out that Alaska regulations require that a wounded bear be dispatched by the guide. If a hunter is absolutely adamant that we don't shoot, that's a little difficult because the law says we should help finish the job if the bear is hit. What we do in that case is avoid shooting if possible, but still not risk letting the bear get away wounded. Clearly, the first shot is worth a hundred times whatever else is going to happen, so shot placement is the key. If it's already dark, we don't go into the woods but come back the next day. For the last five years, we've had the only tracking dog permitted in Alaska, a little Jack Russell terrier. Now regulations in Alaska allow the use of tracking dogs to follow up a wounded bear. It isn't as successful as you might think, though, because often it's rained all night and the scent is cold. The dogs can be helpful, but they're not a complete solution.

What procedure do you follow in tracking a wounded black bear?

Darren DeLuca: I go in by myself first, so I can listen without any interference and try to find the bear that way. Once I'm sure the bear isn't close by, I call in the hunter to stand guard while I do a blood tracking routine.

Mark Galla: Once we've shot, whether we think the bear was hit or not, we go to the spot where the bear was when the hunter fired. We look for any indication—blood, hair, anything—that would signify a hit. If we find the slightest suggestion that the bear was hit, we spend a lot of time looking for it. Even if we're reasonably sure that it was a clean miss, we take a good deal of time looking around to make certain. When we've got a wounded bear, we get another guide or two and we team up to try to find it. If we do find blood, we follow that blood up to the point that it starts to dwindle or disappear. I then leave the others and circle out a couple of hundred yards, looking for the trail. We quite often pick up the blood trail again a good ways out, and that has on many occasions saved us countless hours, and in some cases has led to recovery of the bear when we might not otherwise have found it. To do this you have to leave someone at the last point where you saw definite sign from the bear.

Kevin Olmstead: As I said, the guide goes in first on the trail. It also depends on the abilities of the hunter, but if he's able the hunter goes along with the guide. That way one guy can spot for the other, while one is tracking. As with any wounded animal, it's prudent to be very cautious when following the track.

Jimmie Rosenbruch: We wait for a time and listen to see what's happening. After that, if there's still good light we look for hair or blood. If we don't find any, or if the light is getting poor, we back out of there and return the next morning with all the guides.

A wounded black bear walked these logs to cross the river.

Somebody stands by with a rifle, while several concentrate on tracking. You sometimes get down to a pinpoint of blood every several feet, and even a good bit of blood becomes a precious little bit overnight. A bear is the only animal I know that can walk through wet grass and not leave any tracks at all. They're pretty light travelers for such a big animal. The hunter is invited to go and is welcome, but frankly we'd rather he stay on the beach and let us do our job. The biggest danger is that he represents another firearm in there. I'm sorry to say, but we're not always successful in finding a wounded bear. Again, the key is a methodical, well-placed shot so you kill the animal right there; then you don't have to go through all the tracking.

Chapter 16

SPECIFIC GUIDING AREAS FOR HUNTING BY SPOT-AND-STALK

Describe your home guiding area for black bears, and any distinctions that set it apart.

Darren DeLuca: My area is a chunk of the west coast of Vancouver Island, and we have a lot of rivers and a lot of clear-cut logging. It's fairly steep terrain, relatively remote but accessible. I do ocean-based hunts, too, and also use four-wheel-drive vehicles and quad ATVs for access. It's different from most other areas of North America, but it's fairly typical for outfitters here on the island.

Mark Galla: The area is southeastern Alaska's Inside Passage. There are a number of different islands that I hunt in there. It is set apart from most other bear areas in that the bears here generally grow bigger because they have lots of food available to them. In addition to the usual bear food of berries and forbs and the like, they have fish in abundance. They also forage a lot on the beaches, where they pick up clams and crabs, even barnacles, and whatever other protein they find. These bears don't have to work for a meal because they can just about fall out of bed and get fed. The bears start emerging from their dens in April. They head straight for the beaches because they know there's food there; the shoreline also is the first place free of snow, so the grasses come out first there. Generally, you're going to find more bears in the streams and estuaries at any time of year you're hunting.

Kevin Olmstead: There are about 150 islands altogether in the Queen Charlottes, but we hunt only about four of the larger ones. The biggest distinction is the vegetation and the habitat. There's never a time when food is scarce: berries and salmon in the fall, tender young vegetation in the spring, and big tidal

Scenic lands are one feature of spot-and-stalk bear country.

areas where they can eat crabs and other seafood. The Queen Charlottes are some of the best black bear habitat in the world, with ideal terrain and year-round food sources, everything from high mountains with alpine areas to salmon streams to coastal tidal flats. There was very little hunting going on before we came in, so it was our opportunity to go into an area that was almost untouched for black bear hunting, with only very minimal personal sport hunting being done. Until we started our operation, the only bears shot were problem bears around some of the fishing lodges. In the Queen Charlottes, 50 to 60 percent of the land mass is essentially unhunted territory.

Jimmie Rosenbruch: Our area is indeed set apart. I've hunted around a bit, and the temperate rain forest of southeastern Alaska is different from anywhere else on earth. It's different from a tropical rain forest, and it's certainly different from other areas in North America where black bears are hunted. Here you do very well to find a wounded bear because it's so thick. You can't see far, the bears are very alert, and it's a demanding place to hunt. It's 98 percent clear-cut, and what little remains of the original rain forest is going fast. It might not be around for the next generation to enjoy, so see it while you can.

What kind of terrain is ideal for hunting black bears by the spot-and-stalk method?

Darren DeLuca: Mountainous terrain, like ours, is ideal because you can see across to the opposite slope, or you can gain height and look downward. If the terrain is flat, you just can't see anything. This is the best terrain for finding black bears by spot-and-stalk, but sometimes the stalk can be a real challenge. We hunt a lot of estuaries, working along the ocean, and that can be a lot of fun, too.

Mark Galla: The better beaches aren't so rocky and vertical. They tend to have less pitch and more slope, and there's more grass in such an area, too. Up the estuaries there's quite a bit of grass and more diverse plant life, as well as crustaceans and mussels. The estuaries often have beaches that are really sprawled out, and that's ideal.

Kevin Olmstead: The biggest thing that gives us visibility is the logging that's been done in the Queen Charlotte Islands. There are numerous cut blocks and old logging roads that have been reseeded, and this is all in the midst of optimal bear habitat. You look for natural openings, too, like berry meadows in the alpine areas, tidal flats, salmon streams, and so on. When you get away from such areas, it's so thick that you can't see ten feet.

Jimmie Rosenbruch: The ideal terrain is where you have some visibility. If you can't see very far, you usually can't see the bears. When an area is clear-cut, all the slash is left on the ground, so it's impenetrable by man or beast for about three years. About the third year, you start getting a flush of berries and other growth. For the next eight years or so, it's quite suitable black bear habitat. However, by year ten the conifers start emerging and the canopy closes, creating a biological desert from a habitat standpoint. It takes about eight hundred years to regenerate old growth conditions. All these regrowth areas are a real concern for the game department because they just don't provide the nutrients necessary to sustain black bears, and the biodiversity goes down to about two or three species. In the spring we hunt tidal estuaries because we have a twenty-five-foot tidal variation that keeps those areas free of snow. The big boars come out first, looking for food. In the fall we hunt the salmon creeks, and sometimes we can access some alpine areas above the forests, or large, fairly recent clear-cuts that are just beginning to grow plentiful berries. Because there's no food there, we don't hunt in the forest itself at all.

Describe your typical camp setup and camp routine.

Darren DeLuca: Our main lodge is a fishing lodge that's not being used at the time of year we hunt bears. I move all of my hunters and guides into there, and that's our base of operations. We usually have four hunters at a time.

Mark Galla: The main camp is a fifty-three-foot fiberglass yacht with twin engines. There are three staterooms, and we put two people into each stateroom; the pilot house sleeps three people, and that's me and the crew. The boat has two bathrooms, a full-size shower, and vanities. The salon, which is like a living room in a house, is twelve feet wide by eighteen feet long. All the rooms are quite comfortable and roomy, and most clients are pleasantly surprised by the accommodations and the amenities. The galley in this boat is nicer than the kitchen in most homes. We use two, fourteen-foot welded aluminum skiffs for hunting, one with a forty-horse outboard and the other with a sixty-horse outboard. We can run them with either props or a jet foot. These outfits are what give us access to the best hunting areas, and from them we can find the animals and go ashore to conduct our hunting.

Kevin Olmstead: We have a really nice lodge with ten bedrooms that we built in the Queen Charlottes in 2003. It has all the facilities, including dining, hot water, and the like. Our main spike camps are tent camps or cabins with wood stoves, and these are located in remote areas. It depends to some degree if it's spring or fall. A lot of our spring hunting is done in

Glassing clear-cuts and grassy logging roads is the primary method of hunting on Vancouver Island.

the afternoons and evenings, and we have such long days that time of year that we begin hunting at noon and don't get back to camp until nearly midnight. We then have a late dinner and get to bed. There's no hurry getting up the next morning, though, so it's pretty relaxed. Weather also affects us a lot. If the nights are cold, bears aren't very active in the morning.

Jimmie Rosenbruch: We've got a $4.5 million base camp, with all queen suites and private baths. We stay there every night while we're hunting. If the weather's nice, we take a lunch with us and eat while we're away from the boat. I like hunting bears because we're not getting up in the middle of the night. Hunting from the main boat, we usually leave around 4:00 P.M. and hunt until midnight. We gain about seven minutes of daylight each day in the spring, and we lose about seven minutes a day in the fall. By June, you have shooting light all night long.

These bears are fairly nocturnal, so late evening is the best time to hunt them. Mornings are a waste of time, frankly. You

Trophy Vancouver Island black bear taken by Chris Morris.

get thermal winds off the water in the mornings, so everywhere you go the wind is at your back. In the evening it switches to an offshore flow, so you have the wind advantage then. That's another good reason to hunt evenings.

What is your success rate on trophy animals?

Darren DeLuca: We're virtually 100 percent. There's the odd guy who doesn't get one, usually in the fall, when we sometimes encounter weather problems.

Mark Galla: We could tag people out in the first day or two more than 90 percent of the time, but of course we're looking for that special trophy bear that you don't see every day. I don't think we've ever done a hunt without seeing bears, and we usually see between twenty and seventy-five different bears on a week's hunt. You see fewer bears on the very early hunts, but what you do see then tends to be big boars.

Kevin Olmstead: I always say that it's in the 90-percent range. Just about everybody has multiple opportunities. Only the ones who either can't take advantage of repeated opportunities, or who are holding out for something truly special and don't see what they want, go home without a bear. We really admire hunters who are willing to hold out for a big bear and are willing to go home without one rather than take a small bear.

Jimmie Rosenbruch: It's pretty close to 100 percent, but that depends on your definition of a trophy. For a guy hunting his first bear, any mature bear is a trophy. If he's got several bears and he's looking for something special, sometimes a guy won't see exactly what he wants. A trophy is a very personal thing, and we can meet most hunters' expectations.

Describe your usual hunting method and any common variations.

Darren DeLuca: Early in the spring we go out about 8:00 A.M. and hunt until dark. Later it stays light much longer, so we tend to start later and hunt later. As the season progresses it becomes more of an evening hunt. Very late in the year, late May and early June, the morning hunts are better because it's cool then; we hunt only an hour or two in the late evening just before dark. In the early spring we hunt grassy areas, such as rebuilt logging roads and estuaries on the ocean. As the vegetation progressively greens up the mountain, we use our vehicles to move right up the mountain with it because that's where the bears are. In the fall we hunt primarily on the salmon streams.

Mark Galla: In spring we have long, long days, and we don't get up particularly early most of the time. But in the fall the days are short, and there's less time to hunt. One thing people should realize is that if you can see the shore, you're effectively hunting all the time because someone's always glassing. It's not even necessary to leave the main boat to be looking for bears. In the fall we look to be sure that there are fish in a stream before we go walking up it, and we try to scout it out ahead of time so that we don't wind up in a stream without fish and lose valuable time. In the fall, the wind is usually blowing from the sea and toward the stream. Nearer evening, though, the wind shifts, and we can hunt into the wind. It also depends on the area because there are other areas that require a different approach.

Kevin Olmstead: Most of our area is accessible by four-wheel-drive vehicle via old logging roads and the like. We drive to the best areas and start looking for bears. In the fall we often hunt the salmon streams. We go during the middle of the day and find places where bears are pulling salmon out of the river; you can easily see where they've been active, so you set up behind some cover downwind and just wait for one to come out. It isn't considered baiting if you're waiting at a natural food source like a salmon feeding area or a berry patch.

In the spring we often hunt south-facing slide areas that green up first, where the bears often feed. Logging roads on south slopes do the same thing. We do some hunting from a small aluminum boat in order to access tidal areas where bears may be. The tidal swing is such in the Queen Charlottes that you have to use a small boat so you can move it back to the water if the tide goes out and leaves you high and dry.

Jimmie Rosenbruch: In the spring, as I mentioned, we start hunting in April on the open estuaries that are free of snow and where there's something to eat. At that time of year we spend a lot of time in the skiff. As the season goes on, the feed for the bears gets better, so we start getting out of the skiff and walking and glassing and checking different areas. By mid-May in a normal year, these bears don't move much because they have enough food where they are. Fortunately, about that time the rut kicks in, and you can then have 100 percent success on boars because it's obvious which ones are boars: They're the ones rubbing and traveling and doing their thing.

When fall comes it's much different because we're on rivers looking for bears feeding on salmon. Sometimes we walk, but often we get on a place where we can see well and just glass. These bears are not easy to stalk. The best method is to get ahead of the bear and let him come to you. If a bear is walking in a certain direction, it will rarely turn around and go a different way, so you can cut them off and wait for them to walk by. Often

A real Alaska giant! (Photo courtesy of Mark Galla)

they'll walk within yards of you, especially in the fall when you're set up near a salmon stream.

Which season (spring or fall) offers the best hunting in your area? Early or late in the season?

Darren DeLuca: The spring is an easier hunt, but both spring and fall are about the same quality of bear. The breeding in late May can be an advantage.

Mark Galla: In spring we cover a tremendous amount of territory, and we often spot bears three or four miles away. In fall you're walking up a narrow little stream, so your visibility is limited and you don't see as many bears. However, my preference is the fall because you're up close to the bears and your shots can be as close as thirty or forty feet. Also, there are loads of fish in the streams, and it's an interesting time to be in the wilderness. As far as size is concerned, there's no difference between spring and fall bears. A lot of guys will say that they want to hunt in the fall because the bears are bigger.

Scott Brown's monster Alaska black bear. (Photo courtesy of Jimmie Rosenbruch)

Well, they do weigh more in the fall, naturally, but the size of the wrapper is the same. The skin doesn't get any bigger just because the bear has more fat in the fall.

Kevin Olmstead: Our spring season runs from April 30 to June 30. The fall season runs September 1 to November 30. In the spring we hunt mostly the first of May up into June. In the early part of the spring season it's still too cool for bears to be moving very much. The best time is the middle of May to the middle of June because there's about a month of bear rut during that time, and the boars are actively looking for females. In the fall the best time is the month of September and the first two or three weeks of October because that's when you have salmon in most of the streams. Toward the end of October those bears are slowing down and moving away from areas where they're visible.

Jimmie Rosenbruch: I don't know that one is better than another. Our success is the same, spring or fall. The hunting is different, of course, but I don't think that one time is actually better than another. Our driest month is June and the wettest is October, so that might make some difference to some people. I'd encourage people who really like to bear hunt to try both seasons. If you're on a fall hunt, it's definitely better early because the bears get satiated on fish, which they've been eating all summer, and they may leave the rivers and get harder to find.

Are badly rubbed hides a problem in your area? When is it best to hunt in order to avoid this problem?

Darren DeLuca: After May 21 we start to see some problems with rubbed hides, so we try to get most of our hunts done before that date.

Mark Galla: It's funny, but I've seen some of the worst rubbed hides in the early spring. Bears are still trickling out of their dens up to early June. Certainly you're going to have fewer rubbed bears early than you will as time progresses. In June you're going to have to sort through more bears to avoid bad rubs. The ultimate spring bear has the best coat of all, of course, but rubs can be a problem. On fall bears, rubs are not a problem, but the hair isn't quite as long, either. A good taxidermist can use lofting techniques to make spring and fall bears look exactly the same.

Kevin Olmstead: There's no doubt that the later it gets into the spring the higher the chance of killing a bear that's rubbed. As we get into June, you're going to have to pass up bears because the hide is rubbed. There are times when the hunter has to make the decision whether he wants a big, old bear with a really good skull, or a lesser bear with a pretty hide. We've shot some fantastic bears that have some pretty good rubs on them, yet the skull is close to twenty-one inches. If you're looking for the best hides, you hunt earlier in the spring and later in the fall.

Jimmie Rosenbruch: Late in the spring—say, mid-June on—is the only time this might be a problem. However, a rubbed black bear is very easy to spot. We don't have any color phases. They're all jet black, so anything that isn't jet black is a rub.

Sights of Alaska make every hunt there special. (Photo courtesy of Jimmie Rosenbruch)

There's no problem at all with rubs in the fall. If you do spot a good bear with a rub, you can pass it up, or discuss whether or not it's worth taking.

How much does weather influence hunting success, and how you hunt, in your area?

Darren DeLuca: The biggest single problem is fog, when we lose all visibility and we can't use the boats. Second to that is storms, with wind and rain, which push the bears back into the brush where they tend not to move. Extreme heat does the same thing. If it's only a little rainy or cool, we're out there hunting.

Mark Galla: Weather is important, though I can count on the fingers of one hand all the days we haven't hunted because of weather. As a guide, you've got to get your clients out there for them to have a chance at a bear. There are some days that I wouldn't hunt for myself, but that's not the case. All it takes is for you to skip one day, and, if a guy goes home without a bear, he might say, "Well, we had a lazy guide who didn't want to go out when the weather was a little nasty." I'll do my utmost to get my client out there as long as the weather isn't life threatening. If you get a really heavy, pelting rain, it does hurt the hunting, though. Snow is never an issue.

Kevin Olmstead: In the spring, if it's still cold, the bears just aren't very active, and that makes our hunting more difficult, though our success rate isn't affected. In the fall, the biggest factor is the rain. At that time of year the bears are active pretty much all of the time, so it comes down to a question of what kind of conditions you can actually go out in. Sometimes we have some pretty torrential rainstorms, but we hunt in the rain unless it's just intolerable. That's why good rain gear is such a prime piece of equipment up here. We haven't gone to four-wheelers and the like because when you get wet, you can return to the four-wheel-drive pickup to get warm and dry out until the storm passes.

Jimmie Rosenbruch: If we get heavy rain and big winds, we're done because these bears don't move. It's a rare day when we elect not to hunt at all, but there are days when you can almost predict what's going to happen. A little light rain is actually helpful because it makes everything quieter and it covers your scent to some degree.

Give us your perspective on black bear hunting as a game management tool.

Darren DeLuca: I think it's a valuable tool for reducing the black bear population where it's indicated, particularly near populated areas. However, overall it has a neutral effect on the population because what we take are primarily boars; every time we take one it saves several cubs from being eaten by that bear. For that reason, it's very positive for keeping the population healthy and dynamic.

Mark Galla: One thing is that without hunting, not only would the black bear population suffer, but also the deer population. The older males we try to take are the most efficient predators you can imagine, so taking them out helps younger bears and spares an awful lot of ungulates. We target older males, naturally, because they prey not only on ungulates but also on cubs.

Kevin Olmstead: The biggest factor is to try to harvest older, mature boars. You're taking out some bears that are preying on cubs and young females, so every time you go into an area and take out an old, dominant boar, you increase the cub survival rate significantly. You actually see the overall population of bears increase as a result of hunting these mature boars. By taking only that kind of bear out of one large area, you're not overhunting the area. To reach full potential bears have to get a certain amount of age on them, and they can't do that if you put too much pressure on the population. We take only a fraction of a percentage of the overall population, so we hunt the area very sparingly.

Jimmie Rosenbruch: Black bear permits in Alaska are allocated to outfitters by the U.S. Forest Service after they do the appropriate homework. There's always an overutilization possibility that needs to be watched closely, so we've participated in studies by the Alaska Game Department that allow them to get a better idea of how the bears are faring. In our area black bears are certainly not being overhunted; they have excellent genetics to grow big; and they have superb habitat. As far as hunting them as a management tool goes, I really don't think it's used for population control anywhere. The black bear is a valued resource, though, and they are managed closely by the states and provinces that have them.

Section IV

PARTING SHOTS BY THE BLACK BEAR GUIDES

Chapter 17

FAREWELL FROM THE BLACK BEAR GUIDES

Do you have any unusual hunting stories to share?

Joe Jakab: Back in the late eighties when they opened up Alberta to bait hunting, I went out there to give advice to a resident outfitter friend. We took a jet boat up a river in the north-central part of the province for some eighty miles. It was September, and he had a camp set up for moose and bear. I showed this outfitter where and how to bait. Even though this area is roadless, there are many cut lines made in past winters for oil exploration. Well, after setting up camp, my friend left me and was to return in ten days with clients. I would stay and watch baits and photograph bears. In a few days a bear started coming into camp. He would circle camp, and each night he got bolder and bolder until he eventually came right into it in the late hours of the night. The night before my friend was to return that bear was near my tent all night, and I got very little sleep.

The next morning my friend and three clients arrived. I had slept in on account of the bear keeping me up all night. I told everyone about the bear, and I decided to sleep some more while everyone took a cruise upriver to look for moose. I was sleeping soundly when all of a sudden something hit me pretty hard through the canvas of the tent. Right away I thought that a hunter had sneaked back into camp and was playing bear with me. I walked out of the tent, and there was a very large bear walking around a smoldering campfire. I couldn't believe it. I thought about shooting it, but I figured that this would be an easy bear for one of the clients. I was wrong! Everyone saw the tracks and the muddy prints on the side of the tent, but that bear never came back again.

Horace Lane: Some four years ago I had a Norwegian hunter named Rune Orbeck on a spring bear hunt, and he had been

Glassing for black bears on Vancouver Island.

returning every season. In 2006 he returned again with a fellow Norwegian named Rune Aasberg. In addition to being Norwegian, they also shared common occupations as electrical contractors with very successful businesses back home. Through their businesses they were part of the same professional association of electrical contractors in Norway. One of their association conventions had been held in France, and over dinner Orbeck had discussed with Aasberg his many exciting trips to Newfoundland and his bear hunts with Riverrun Outfitters. Orbeck had hunted successfully with me several times, but the stories he told after returning from the stand in the evenings were never about the kill but rather about what he had experienced: How bears would approach, how those magnificent animals would slip silently through the green woods, and how the largest of them would rarely come to the bait but would sit so close, just out of sight but near enough that he could hear them breathing. He'd describe how they would exhale (blow) a warning to the other, smaller bears that dinner was being served—but that it was all theirs, so stay away! Rune could imitate the sound extremely well as he related every detail of the hunt. We would all wait for Rune to return in the evening with great anticipation of the evening's events. Those nights at camp were memorable for us all. It was the telling of such stories at that dinner that had sparked Aasberg's interest in coming to Newfoundland. Aasberg had hunted nothing bigger than birds, but on a handshake they agreed to come together to hunt black bear here.

Aasberg, like many Norwegians, is a very adventurous fellow. Three or four years before he had been to Newfoundland as part of a yearlong journey on a forty-three-foot sailboat with his wife and two children. They had sailed west to Iceland and Greenland, then south to the coast of Labrador, and on to St. John's, Newfoundland. They had then gone as far south as Venezuela before returning home. Rune Aasberg is a very competent sailor, and this year he is part of the Norwegian crew in international matches. For their hunt here, they arrived a few days early to do some sightseeing. I set them up with one of my guides to do some trout fishing and to check some baits in the process. Their interest in fishing passed very quickly, however, when they saw the activity on the baits, and they started hunting that night. Orbeck was put on a bait way back in the country next to an old skidder road, while Aasberg was put on a stand approximately six miles away. We knew that the baits were active from observations by our main guide, Wade Nicholas.

That season hunters were allowed two bears per license for the first time in ten years. The camp rule is one bear per license, but for a trophy fee you are permitted to take a second. I had advised Aasberg of this policy and suggested that, this being his first big-game hunt, he just take a decent bear and not wait for something special. Wade settled both hunters and waited for the radio silence to break, having every confidence that both would see bears. Sure enough, two and a half hours later Aasberg called to say that he had shot a bear. Wade was within earshot and had heard the single shot ring out. Little did he know what a magnificent animal it turned out to be. Wade and Aasberg tried to get the bear out of the woods themselves, but to no avail. We had to call in three other people to get the animal out! It weighed more than four hundred pounds, with a skull green scored close to twenty-one inches. What a trophy!

Orbeck stayed on the stand until dusk and had a very exciting evening, seeing three bears, including one exceptionally big one that did not give him an opportunity for a shoot. He was always the most patient of hunters and saw and heard more bears than any hunter in camp. This hunt was to prove no different. He saw that giant bear two times over the next four nights, and we determined that some modifications to the stand were necessary; the bear was circling around back and was able to see Orbeck in the stand. We made the necessary changes to the stand and waited a night to rest it before going back to hunt. Orbeck had seen several smaller bears there, but it was the big one he was after. Sure enough, the plan worked. The big guy came in early, and Orbeck made the first shot count. Knowing that he could take two bears he decided to wait it out and see what else might show up. Within forty minutes a second animal came in, not quite as big, but he took that one as well. This was the first time in my operation we've had one hunter take two bears the same evening. The bigger bear also weighed over four hundred pounds. Orbeck and Aasberg share a common first name, country, occupation, favorite restaurants, and now the

Fully furred trophy black bear from Vancouver Island.

experience of hunting black bear in Newfoundland. One came as a stranger to me, but they both left as friends, with thoughts of returning again to this island that reminds them a little of home.

Don Lind: There are so many things that happen each spring that I wish I had started writing them down so I could remember them all. One particular incident does stand out, though. It was week three of a busy spring season, and I had put my hunters into their stands and was doing my bait run. I had a tub of bait, a beaver carcass, and a barrel strapped into the back of my Argo. I was traveling down a south-facing line on a clear, hot day with the sun in my face, and it wasn't long before I started to nod off. I decided to take advantage of the warmth and solitude and stopped the Argo in the middle of the cut line for a quick nap. I was soon stretched out across the front seat with my feet hanging out of the Argo on one side and my head on my jacket on the other.

I guess I had slept for about a half-hour when I was awakened by what I thought was someone beating on the barrel in the back of the Argo. Not wanting whoever it was to think that they were going to startle me, I sat upright quickly and let out a holler. Sitting in the back seat of the Argo was a two-year-old black bear, staring at me. I'm sure it was more shocked than I, but I wish someone had come around the corner just then and witnessed the scene. The startled bear, not wanting to miss out on an opportunity, grabbed the beaver carcass by the tail and bolted out of the Argo. When it landed on the ground the bear stepped on the dragging end of the beaver, tripped itself up, and dropped the beaver. It regained its composure, though, picked up the beaver, and charged off into the brush. It all happened so fast that I never left the front seat of the Argo.

Claude Turcotte: Every year there's one story after another. Two years ago, we had a bow hunter on a stand, a repeat client who was a very good hunter. We knew that there was a big bear in the area. A young bear came to the bait, saw him on the stand, and came right over to him and climbed the tree! All night there were four bears right in front of him, as well as the one climbing the tree. He had to poke the bear with the arrow, but it wasn't scared at all. He finally picked the best bear and shot it, hoping that would scare the others off. He killed the bear, but it didn't scare the others.

When the guides came, they whistled to the hunter. The rule is that if you know there's a bear around, you don't answer back. He didn't answer. They took the baiting trail to the site, talking and making their usual noise, so the bears wouldn't think much about their coming in; they're pretty well used to it. When they arrived at the bait, the big bear jumped on a forked tree and sat there popping his jaws at them. They had to hold that bear on the forked tree with a stick. Everybody just kind of backed all the way to the truck, with the bear following all the way.

Wade Lemon: I've got a doctor friend from Ohio who hunts quite a lot with us. We had run a bear into its den, a hole that dropped straight down about three feet and then went on back from there, and there was a big boulder just toward the back of the den. The dogs were in there barking like crazy. We crawled in far enough to catch all the dogs and pull them back out. We didn't have a flashlight, but we managed to get all of the dogs out. My friend had a video camera with a little bitty light on it. I stepped down in there and turned it on, and that bear was right there, where you could almost touch him, just lying still.

We figured that my friend could get up above the rock, and with his .44 Magnum pistol he could shoot it. So he went up there and got into position, and of course there was no place for me to go. I could only get as tight to the ground as I could because I knew that bear was coming right over me. The doctor was getting ready to shoot, and I was thinking, boy, this is nuts! He fired, and nothing happened. He fired again, and the bear came boiling out of that hole, right over the top of me, and went out in the direction of a different sliver of daylight than the one we'd come in by. It left through a crevice.

We couldn't tell if we'd done any damage, but we could hear the dogs rolling out of there after that bear. I told my friend that he must have hit that bear pretty well, and surely the dogs would have it bayed shortly. We turned and started to go out the hole we'd come in by, and all of a sudden we heard the dogs coming back toward us! We were still down in the hole, so the pack had to be pretty close for us to hear them. About that time, that bear came back into the hole, right on top of us, because the dogs had chased him back home. Things got pretty wild at that point. My friend opened up on him like a Wild West gunfighter, blazing away—and he finally got him.

Jerry "Finn" Nykanen: We'd treed a bear during the preseason, when we were just training dogs. The bear came down the tree to several feet from the ground, and a hound jumped up and grabbed it by the butt and clamped down hard. That bear climbed back up the tree about twenty feet, with the dog swinging like a pendulum, or like a piece of meat. When it got as high as it was going, it reached back and brushed that dog off like a fly, and boy did that dog hit the ground! Unfortunately, we didn't even get any pictures because we were all standing there with our mouths open. The other dogs jumped on the one that had fallen and worked him over, thinking it was the bear coming down.

Mike Richie: I often hunt with some friends, Terry and Bill, in the spring here in Idaho. Some years ago we went over to the coast in Washington to hunt. I was working as a sawyer that summer, and on Friday after work we took off for the coast and drove all night to get there. It was about 7:00 A.M. when we met up with the rest of our group, and we didn't even sleep; we just took off hunting. We got on a big bear right away, and that bear ran all day. He would bay up, but before we could get there he'd take off again. Then he'd tree, but before we could get to the tree, he'd bail out and take off again. I had my boy with me, and he was about seven years old. We had lost the dogs, and even though we had tracking collars on them, we couldn't get a good signal. I told everybody to stay put while I climbed the ridge to try to get a better signal. When I got up there, though, I could hear the dogs treed close by.

I yelled to the guys to come on up, but before they got there the bear bailed out again and took off. It treed again not too far away. We moved to that tree, and as we came up to it the bear was coming down again, to make another run. We yelled to our shooter, Terry, to shoot the bear, and he made a terrific shot. The big animal hit the ground. None of the dogs were tied back, so Bill jumped in and grabbed one of them with his left hand while he reached for his pistol and another dog with the right. He was going to make sure the bear was dead by shooting it in the head. While he was wrestling with the dogs, Terry stepped up and shot the bear again. Bill immediately hit the ground. He said, "Terry, you shot me! My leg's broken!"

I looked, expected to see a big old .454 hole in him, but he wasn't bleeding at all. Terry's not the kind of shooter who makes a mistake like that. I was really puzzled now, since Bill had obviously been shot.

I pulled up his pants leg, and it almost looked as if the bear had bitten him. You could see where the bullet had scraped along his leg and gone in at the top of his boot. It had entered his shin and broken both leg bones going in and again coming out, before lodging just above his ankle. Terry was looking, too, and he said, "Bill! You shot yourself!" Bill, of course, denied it until we opened his pistol and found a spent round in the chamber. What had happened was that when he was reaching for the dogs he had his finger on the trigger. When Terry fired, the dogs jumped. Bill had flinched, and his gun had gone off. We were about three miles from the road, so we had a problem.

We doubled up a meat sack and put it around his heel and around the side of his leg, and we made a makeshift splint to immobilize the leg. We had another guy we called "Big Daddy" down in the pickup. He drove a truck in that country and knew it really well, so I headed on back to see if he could get the truck any closer in. I hit a good trail not far from the accident site, then cut across country back to the vehicle. Big Daddy knew exactly where that trail came out. When we got back I cut willow sticks and fixed up some crutches. Bill made it most of the way to the truck on his own, though we did have to carry him maybe a half-mile. We got some good pictures of him and the bear, with Terry holding the bear by the ears and me holding Bill by the ears!

Darren DeLuca: This is a story that happened ten or twelve years ago on the north side of Vancouver Island. I was up there with a hunter, and we saw a big bear back in an estuary. We sneaked up so we could get a better look, but we couldn't actually see the bear very well. My hunter was shooting a .375, and I was carrying my .338. I kept telling him not to fire until we could get the animal up and see how big he was. The hunter kept asking me over and over how big the bear was.

When the bear finally started to get up—and before I could tell anything about its size—the guy fired and hit it, but the bullet struck way too far back. We went over for a look, and we could sure tell that the shot was off; we found chunks of intestine. I knew that this was going to be a long day. We waited about twenty minutes, and then we started following the trail. I had the hunter stay about fifty yards behind me, and we got on the blood trail, where I was finding various bear parts. It was pretty easy going at first because we were under some old growth forest and the blood trail was obvious. We then got up into a windfall with trees lying every which way, and the tracking got a lot harder. We went up and down and over and around, and finally we got through the windfall. That was good, but the bad part was that we then got into incredibly thick brush with bear trails laced all through it. It was so thick that the trails were like giant mouse holes, and we had to get onto our hands and knees to get through. I started following the bear, crawling a little

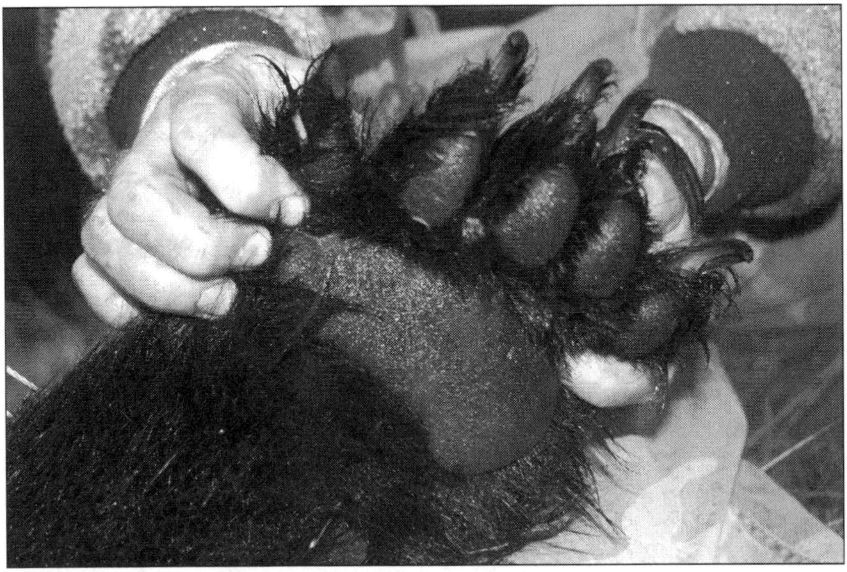

A big bear has a very big foot.

and pushing my gun ahead, crawling some more and pushing my gun ahead again. There were a lot of cross-trails, all of them so well worn that it looked as though bears had been using them for hundreds of years. I stayed on the blood trail for several hundred yards, and I finally reached a little clearing where I could actually stand up. I got up, stretched, turned, and looked—and the bear was coming right at me!

I tried to get the gun up, but there was just no way. He was coming so quickly and the brush wouldn't let me move. The bear leaped up at me, and went right for my face! I think that bears tend to go for each other's eyes when they fight, and that's exactly what this one went for on me. I threw my gun up and fought with the bear, but it was so darned thick in there that he couldn't knock me down. He did knock my gun away, though, and he scratched up my face and chest pretty bad. Then he ran away up one of the tunnels. My blood was up now, so I grabbed my gun and took off after him, figuring it was so tight that he couldn't turn around in there, so maybe I could get a shot at him. I chased him as far and as fast as I could, and I did get glimpses of him in front of me. Finally, he wheeled off and went up a side trail and disappeared.

At that point I decided the best course of action was just to get out of there and come back with a better plan. We returned to camp, got some bear dogs, and turned them loose in there. They found the bear about 150 yards up the trail, stone dead; that attack had been its last gasp. I saw my wife a few days later, and she thought that a stick or something had scratched me. Word finally got back to her, though, and fortunately I wasn't at home at the time to take the heat. The only thing that saved me was that the brush had been so thick the bear couldn't knock me down. If he'd gotten me down, I'd have been toast.

Mark Galla: I've got a couple I probably shouldn't tell. But one that comes to mind involves a couple of German guys I had in camp and a guide from up north who comes by every year. It was a spring hunt, and we had spotted a really good bear down the shore. The guide got the hunters into the skiff, and they headed out and got downwind of the bear, sneaked up on it, and took the shot. The bear ran up into some very steep terrain that pitched straight down into what was essentially a fjord.

Close to the edge of the shore the water was extremely deep. We were searching for the bear when all of a sudden there was a commotion, and one of the hunters exclaimed, "The bear, the bear—it went into the water!"

I didn't see the bear hit the water, but there were certainly lots of ripples, as if something had hit it. I could see the guide and the other hunter looking into the water, their eyes as big as saucers. It seems that one of them had found the bear and given it a kick to move it a little, and the kick had had more effect than they anticipated. The thing came alive and leaped into the water! Well, spring bears don't float—and fall bears more or less don't, either—so the bear went down. I sent the guide back with the skiff and halibut rods and jigs, and soon there they were, fishing for bear! It didn't take long to hook it, but it sure took a while to land it.

Jimmie Rosenbruch: About twenty years ago we were hunting on Prince of Wales Island, where we don't hunt anymore. It was springtime, and we'd cruised in the skiff up into a little estuary and spotted a bear. It was a really nice bear, and it was standing out in the open in some alders, fully visible, looking at us. I thought, man, that's really unusual that a bear would just stand there and not run away immediately. Well, it was certainly a very good bear, so we eased up closer and shot it. When we walked over to it, we found that it had been caught by one foot in a cable snare. It was a giant black bear, more than 8 feet, and it had dug up a huge mound of dirt trying to get loose. I'd never seen anything like it before, and haven't since. We considered it fair chase because we had no idea that it was caught. We reported it to the game department, of course, and they didn't know anything about how that snare got there. Anyway, that hunter could sure say I had one tied up for him!

What is the most dangerous situation you or your hunters have encountered hunting black bears? What was the outcome? Why did it occur, and how could it have been avoided?

Joe Jakab: I can't recall a really dangerous situation. If you do things right, you can avoid them.

Horace Lane: We once had a situation involving cubs that was pretty dangerous. A lady was out hunting with one of my guides, and two cubs had come to the bait and were milling around. All of a sudden the mother bear came over the hill and charged the stand, snapping her teeth and frothing at the mouth, really threatening the hunter and guide. The hunter just froze and was unable to react. The guide took the rifle from her, though fortunately he didn't have to use it. But it was surely a nerve-racking moment. The bear finally left when the cubs took off. The lady did go out hunting for the rest of the week, and she finally took a nice bear.

Don Lind: The most dangerous situation always has to be tracking wounded bears. Over the years we've had a couple of wounded bears charge us, and we've followed some to den sites. On only one occasion was the situation so dangerous that anyone was at risk. This was a couple years ago, and I was filming a repeat hunter. The hunter made what we thought at the time was a perfect lung shot with his bow on a large bear.

We were in a hurry to retrieve the bear with adequate light for filming, so we took up the trail immediately without bringing a rifle for backup; after all, we thought that bear wasn't going very far. After a lengthy tracking job in fading light I came across the bear lying on its side in dense undergrowth just on the edge of the trail. Without walking up to the downed bear I immediately hailed the hunter and started filming the approach.

As the hunter was narrating and walking up to his trophy, the bear got up and charged from only about ten yards. I guess I was the first thing the bear saw, and it took out after me, leaving the hunter standing and watching. The bear was fatally wounded and charged only a short distance, about ten yards, and then stopped. I had also stopped, still filming, and turned back to see the bear now standing only scant feet from the hunter. I started moving closer to the bear and making noises, to keep its attention on me so the hunter could move away. But the bear picked up the hunter's movement and took after him, chasing him around a large spruce tree. This charge was very short, though, only a few yards, and the bear stopped again. A second arrow quickly finished it off. Although we did get some incredible footage out of it, the situation put both of us at risk because we were more concerned about film quality than proper retrieval of the bear. It was an important lesson learned, and we were fortunate it turned out the way it did.

Claude Turcotte: That incident about the young bear climbing the tree might be it, but something like that happens every year.

Wayne Bosowicz: I've almost been shot several times. As far as the bear itself, when it comes down the tree, if you're not set up properly you can sure get run over. The bear usually has in his eye exactly where he wants to go, and nothing will change his mind. He'll go right through you if you're in the way, just to get into a thicket or some other place. You don't know that, though, and it will sure get your heart beating if he comes your way. It's the same thing with the dogs if they're loose. The bear gets one dog on his mind, and he's going to go after that particular one and ignore all the others. I don't know why that

Alaskan coastal rain forest—home of huge black bears. (Photo courtesy of Jimmie Rosenbruch)

is, but I've lost dogs to bears with that mindset. I've had a few come right over me, leaving me with questions as to whether they were after me or just getting away. If they start popping their teeth in front of you, though, you've got trouble.

Wade Lemon: We had a big bear we were chasing, and I had a rifle hunter with me. We'd managed to get ahead of the bear, and the hunter had got off a shot and hit it in the knee, which kind of broke it down a bit. The bear turned and kept on fighting the dogs, so the hunter fired again, and this time the shot went in the chest, but too low to kill it quickly. The bear headed down a big, rough canyon away from us, and shortly we could hear the dogs baying him. It was up on a treacherous ledge, and it took us an hour to crawl over to it. When we got there, the dogs had run that bear into a den. I couldn't talk the hunter into going in and looking, and we didn't have a flashlight. Well, somebody had to finish the job, so I crawled in the hole.

I got over to one side to let in what little light was there, and I could kind of see the bear. I couldn't tell which end was which, though, and the bear was growling and popping his teeth. I studied the situation a while, and I finally figured out which end was the head. I crawled out and told the hunter the situation, and where to shoot the bear. He was carrying a scoped rifle, and I told him it was going to be almost like shooting by Braille. He just wouldn't go in, though, so I took the rifle and told him to hold onto my feet while I went down in. I told him that the second he heard the gun go off he was to pull me out as fast as he could. Well, we got everything lined out, and I crawled down into the hole with the gun. All of a sudden, the gun barrel went flying to one side: The bear had hit it hard with his paw! Things were now getting pretty tense. I pulled the gun back into position, figured out where I thought the neck was, and pulled the trigger. The hunter was a big, stout boy, and, man, did he drag me out of that hole—and drag all the skin off my chin in the process! I got out just about the time the bear's head came through the hole. Fortunately, he was dead, but it was sure kind of scary there for a while. You'll notice that I listed a flashlight as one of the most important things a guy can bring on a bear hunt.

Mike Richie: The worst thing that ever happened was one time when a hunter was walking the trail ahead of us; he saw a bear and took a shot. He actually shot the bear in the foot. There was blood everywhere when I arrived. I'd left my own pistol back in camp for some reason that day. I cut the dogs loose, though, and they bayed the bear in a big brush pile; I could climb up on top of the pile and see it. The hunter's bullet had struck the back foot, so the bear was still plenty mobile. I'd instructed the hunter to stay put when the bear bayed up, so there I was, with no weapon and a wounded bear. I was kind of young and foolish back then, so I tried to get up on top of the brush pile and hit the bear in the head with a rock. Every time I'd climb up the bear would come charging out, but the dogs would be on it in a second and run it back in the brush. I finally saw how dangerous this was. I went back and got the hunter, and we killed it with the firearm. A wounded bear in the brush is about as bad as it gets. I don't think I've ever left my pistol behind since then.

Darren DeLuca: I guess the incident I described above is the tightest situation I was ever in. I learned that bears can move much faster than you might think. That attack happened so fast I hardly had time to think about it until it was over. On another point, wounded bears late at night are really a predicament. That happens sometimes, and you tend to stay a little later than you should; you can be way back in the timber, and it can be pretty dangerous.

Mark Galla: I've had a couple of hairy situations develop, but not many. A few years ago one of my hunters with another guide had shot a bear on an old logging road, and it had plunged off into the thick underbrush. We all got together to track this wounded bear, which always happens in the last light of day. As I usually do, I kept them working the main blood trail while I got out ahead to try to save some time. I jumped the bear a couple of times but couldn't get a shot. It crossed a stream, and then another, and by that time we were using headlamps because it was now completely dark. I got into one of those areas where there's so much bear sign you can't tell which is the right bear. I decided to run on ahead and try to get in front of the animal. I stepped up over the top of knoll, and the bear jumped up right in front of me and disappeared into thick brush. I got off two shots, but neither of them connected.

I ran to where I thought the bear had gone, and after a few seconds I stopped on a small rise and listened. I should have been able to hear him crashing through the brush, but there was dead silence—no commotion of any kind. It was weird, and to this day I don't know exactly why that bear did what he did. I thought, well, maybe I hit him, but I didn't know. For some reason I stuck my rifle barrel down into the brush below me, shone the light, and there was the nose of the bear, only inches from my foot! Had I not looked, my next course of action would have been to jump off that rise and head where I thought he'd gone. If I had, I'd have lit literally on top of him! No doubt I would have been bitten badly, at the very best. I don't think he would have killed me, but who knows? He was mortally wounded, but he was certainly far from dead at the time.

Kevin Olmstead: We haven't had any dangerous situations so far. We've been very fortunate in that regard. We have had the situation develop a couple of times in which bears have been pretty aggressive in trying to take over a Sitka black-tailed deer kill from a hunter. It's never developed into anything serious, but it can make you nervous.

Jimmie Rosenbruch: You know, I've never found an animal on the planet that's aggressive; it's just not their nature. I've had some run toward us after the shot; it looks like a charge, but it really isn't. They're just heading for the nearest cover. The most dangerous situations we've encountered have involved not the bear but the weather. Environmental conditions are far more threatening than animals. We've had a few people get hurt over the years, but it's never involved a bear. It's always something else.

What do you see as the most critical environmental/management/public relations issues affecting the future of hunting black bears?

Joe Jakab: Spring bear hunting was closed in Ontario in 1999, the deed accomplished by a wealthy businessman putting pressure on the premier prior to elections. Ontario has a population of about nine million people, and most of them live in large cities like Toronto, within one hundred miles of the U.S. border. As in most places in the world, urban populations have little knowledge of wildlife and hunting, and people make decisions on the basis of emotion and not reality. All hunting and gun rights are taking flak. Spring bear hunting and especially hunting over bait are easy targets because even hunters are divided to some degree over those hunts. I think that we as hunters need to do our best to explain why we hunt, and that it is a love of the outdoors more than anything else. To hunt is to become educated in the pursuit of animals, and to be involved with the natural world. If nonhunters understood that hunters really do respect the wild lands and animals, and if they

Near day's end hunting black bears on Vancouver Island.

understood why people like to hunt, perhaps it would do a lot to keep the general public on our side.

Horace Lane: In Newfoundland we've traditionally been a target for antihunting groups because we're few in number. Black bear hunting over bait has been a tempting target for antihunters for a long time, and we've got to educate the public that it's the only way we can effectively hunt bears in this part of the world.

Don Lind: I think that the most serious threat to bear hunting in our area is the antibaiting or the antispring hunt movement that has shut down those hunts in other regions. As is usually the case with antihunters, they work on people's emotions and ignore the biological evidence. We have such a large population of bears in our region that if it's not kept under control by effective hunting methods, the animals become a serious nuisance and are destroyed, and totally wasted, by those whose property rights or economic well-being is being infringed on. Also, in more than ten years of spring bear hunting we have never orphaned a spring cub. That is another great aspect of baiting. The bears are brought in close, and confirmation can be made if the bear is a sow with cubs.

Claude Turcotte: Shooting small bears, or sows and cubs, makes for very bad publicity. We've got to keep up the kill rate for big bears and stay away from killing the immature ones.

Wayne Bosowicz: Lack of public knowledge about bears and bear hunting in general is a problem. It doesn't matter if it's over bait or with dogs, the public has serious misconceptions.

Too many people assume, for example, that you just get a pack of dogs and go out and kill a bear. That's so far from the truth. They also think that bait hunting is simple. The only ones who think that are people who've never done it. I've participated in legislative hearings since the early 1970s, and I pose this question to people, "Just what was it that you didn't like about your bear hunt that makes you feel the way you do?" You know how many opponents of bear hunting have ever been bear hunting? Zero. None. They have no idea what bear hunting is like. We just won a major victory to keep our bear hunt in Maine. It cost us $1.7 million, but we won. What did it was our campaign to educate the public. Maine has one of the longest, most reputable black bear studies in the world, and we've got plenty of impeccable data. It was our incredible state biologists who really were responsible for the win.

Wade Lemon: There's been a lot of pressure to outlaw hunting bears, especially with dogs. It isn't right because it's one of the few kinds of catch-and-release hunting you can do, especially for bears. How else can you capture the animal, determine its size and sex, and let it go if it's not the bear you want? I think it's a public relations problem, letting people know what we do, and the reasons why dog hunting for bears is highly ethical and right. There's a misconception, too, that a guy can wait until he's old to do a hound hunt for bears because all that happens is that the hounds chase the bear up a tree, and you walk up and shoot it. That does happen, but it's more often the most challenging and rewarding hunt a guy can go on. There are just so many variables to take into account—the dogs, the bear, the terrain, the weather, and so on.

Jerry "Finn" Nykanen: I just don't understand how the Department of Natural Resources comes up with figures when it comes to determining numbers of tags to allocate. They've got a bunch of kids out counting bear scat, and they don't have any idea what they're doing. Most of them have never seen a bear. They're so far off on their bear count that they aren't even close. Officially, there are between twelve thousand and fourteen thousand bears in Wisconsin, and I'm certain that there are twenty-five thousand. We're even seeing bears down here where there used to be none. We can't run dogs right here where I live; you've got to go north of Highway 8. They're only issuing one thousand tags in the area where we hunt, and there used to be as many as two thousand.

Mike Richie: You know, the environmentalists are trying to shut down bear hunting with hounds because they think it's unsportsmanlike. I've done a few videos, and I've gotten a lot of calls from the antihunters, cussing me out and calling me names but refusing to listen to our side of it. When you try to explain why hound hunting is good sport they hang up on you, so it's a pretty one-sided debate. I have a standing offer to anybody who thinks hound hunting is unsportsmanlike: They're invited to come hunting with me, and if they still think it's unsportsmanlike they don't owe me a thing. I've even had deer hunters and people who hunt bears over bait tell me that hound hunting is unsportsmanlike, even though they've never tried it. They should give it a try before making such a judgment. You follow those hounds far enough and you find out pretty quickly that it's the ultimate in sportsmanship, as far as bear hunting is concerned. That's especially true in the Selway, where the country is so rough; we get outrun more than 50 percent of the time and never tree or bay the bear.

Darren DeLuca: I think the biggest problem is that bears are easily personified by the news media as furry and cute animals. It's really easy for them to corrupt what bears really are, so it's an easy sell to the public to limit or eliminate bear hunting. It's not particularly a meat hunt, like hunting deer and elk, where people go out and fill their freezers. It's very much a trophy hunt, so I believe that it's quite vulnerable from that perspective. It's a matter of hunters and outfitters behaving ethically because if we don't, we get killed in the public relations arena.

Mark Galla: I get the question a lot about how many bears we can shoot. Well, here in my area you can take only one bear. The next question is, "Why do you charge such-and-such, when I can go to Canada and shoot two bears for a lot less?" Well, for one thing, I'm using a $500,000 boat with all the accessories while the competition is using a Ford pickup and a bucket of doughnuts. Also, operations that offer two bears usually take small bears, not really trophies. The bears don't get a chance to grow up. For one thing, on cheaper hunts, they have to run a lot more hunters through, and take a lot more bears, and those bears aren't necessarily mature. The one-bear limit certainly helps to make sure that bears have a chance to grow to their potential.

I hate to mention another thing because it sounds so self-serving, but there are a lot of outfitters up here who are so-called transporters. They can't assist in the hunt for a bear in any way. They can't even show a bear on the beach to a hunter because at that point they're essentially guiding. What they run isn't a bear hunt, but a floating hotel. They can take guys in, give them a skiff or a ride to the beach, and the hunters are then on their own. The problem is that they generally take a lot more guys, and they try to crowd them into smaller quarters. I never touched transporting, even before I was a licensed guide because you're turning guys loose who may not even know how to operate an outboard motor—and they're certainly not familiar with the area they're hunting, where tides can fluctuate by up to twenty-five feet.

The last thing is that do-it-yourself hunters generally don't know a big bear from a cub. Even with all the experience we've got, we still make occasional bad calls. Also, a lot of them will shoot a bear, and nine out of ten bears are going to make it to the brush after the shot. The majority of these hunters are not going into the brush after a major predator, but instead they leave that one and go after another. The same thing happens if they shoot a small bear—the temptation is to kick it into the brush and go after a larger one. The thing is that there's no control on their activities, and they probably lose 50 percent or more of the bears they hit, either because they won't adequately follow up or because they bury and forget the little guy. I hate to bring it up because as I say, it sounds self-serving, but in my opinion, nonresidents should be required to have a guide for black bears. Even people of limited means would be better off hunting bears with a guide because they'll have a better, safer experience, and they'll most likely kill a bigger bear, even if they have to save an extra year or two to be able to afford it.

Kevin Olmstead: I think that the perception of the public is so very important. Many people who don't hunt are unaware that we have a very sustainable population. With the management that we do, our bear population is actually increasing because of the successful hunting program. That's the opposite of what the antihunting groups are telling the public, and it's our job to educate the public on the truth of the matter.

Jimmie Rosenbruch: Habitat protection is the key, without a doubt, in our part of the world. Black bears will cohabit with humans, which brown bears won't, but they've got to have a place to live. Alaska is very serious about its black bears, but many other states aren't. We also need to do everything we can to reduce the harvest of females.

Do you have any parting words of wisdom for black bear hunters?

Joe Jakab: While on a safari with Robin Hurt in Tanzania, I sat in a blind with him and my best friend, Carl Hilbert. I witnessed Carl shooting a lion and later a leopard. In taking the leopard, we were out nine times before he got his opportunity, but it was a time of extreme anticipation and excitement. Carl commented that waiting on the leopard, and then waiting to get his shot, was one of the most intense experiences he's ever had. When it was over, I told Carl that it was the same way when you're waiting for a black bear to come to the bait—that familiar, intense sensation I've come to know so well. He found out last fall in Ontario, and although a black bear isn't as glamorous as a leopard, the experience can still be intense. If you haven't tried a baited bear hunt, you're missing a thrill.

Horace Lane: Don't stay on the stand too late because that's when most mistakes are made. You might miss a good bear, or kill the wrong bear, and you won't always get a second chance. A shot that's not well placed can cost you a bear. We have a policy in place that if the hunter draws blood, the hunt is over, so it's really important to make a good shot. You don't have a license to kill, you have a license to hunt. If you wound an animal and it escapes, you should walk away from it and consider that one your animal.

Don Lind: I think that baited bear hunts, particularly in the spring, are a hunt that may often be overlooked by many hunters. It does not need to be a boring stand hunt without seeing bears if you do your research and book in the right region with a reputable outfitter. Check with several references and pay the price for a quality hunt. Many of my hunters have seen more bears on the first night on one of our stands than on several hunts in other regions.

Claude Turcotte: Shooting small bears, or sows and cubs, is very bad for the public perception. We've got to keep up the kill rate for big bears and stay away from killing the immature ones.

Wayne Bosowicz: As black-bear dog hunters, we have got to get rid of any chip on our shoulders and start supporting each other. We're all hunters, and I'm personally tired of the low-key approach, such as bringing in the word "harvest" to soften what we do. I'm sick of such words. I don't "harvest" bears, I go out and kill them. "Harvest" is one of those words I'm starting to hate, like "green" and "global." But we've certainly got to stick together as hunters, work with our state game and fish departments, and do everything we can to increase public knowledge because that's the only way we'll ultimately prevail.

Wade Lemon: The most important thing is to find a track so you know what you're chasing with dogs. It's also very important to have the dogs in shape because if you try to chase a bear with tender-footed dogs, you'll blow the pads off their feet right away. It takes two weeks to heal them up, and by then bear season is over. Another thing is to use enough dogs to get the job done. You can get a bear with just a few dogs, but I see a lot of days when I'm glad I took twenty.

Jerry "Finn" Nykanen: Go up and see the guy before you

Michael Price's great Vancouver Island trophy black bear.

go hunting with him, if possible. Make sure you're comfortable with him, and see what kind of operation he's got. He might be one of those guys who's taking people out to sit, and they're shooting bears that weigh barely a hundred pounds.

Mike Richie: If you've never tried it with hounds, give it a try. People either love it or hate it, but it's a true challenge, and something any serious hunter should try at least once.

Darren DeLuca: Whether you're doing it on your own or with a guide, go where there are bears! It's the old saw of hunting ducks or deer where ducks or deer live, so you can be successful in finding them. Also, when you get an opportunity, it's of paramount importance to take great care with your shot.

Mark Galla: Be aware that hunting is hunting, and it's not a guarantee. All that a guide can guarantee is a better shot at taking a bear, and he can give the client a quality experience. There are too many positive things that can happen on a hunt to base all the success or failure on whether or not you kill a bear.

Kevin Olmstead: Hunting black bears is one of the most thrilling and adventurous hunts you can go on today. We think that's especially true up in the Queen Charlotte Islands, with the raw beauty of spectacular scenery combined with the joy of hunting the largest black bears in the world in their natural habitat.